The Norman and Phyllis Show

A Memoir
About Crazy Parents

Joel Dubin

About the Author

Joel Dubin is a retired cybersecurity consultant turned humor author. This book, *The Norman and Phyllis Show*, is a memoir about his eccentric parents, the source of his sense of humor.

His most recent book, *The 7 Habits of Highly Dysfunctional Companies*, is based on decades of consulting work for screwed up companies around the world. He survived the corporate world with his sanity intact, though that is still debatable.

His book, *Yes Dear! A Husband's Guide to Marriage*, is based on experiences from his over thirty years of marriage and the lesson Norman taught me about his own marriage to Phyllis: your wife is always right.

He speaks several foreign languages, including fluent gibberish. He is a graduate of Columbia Graduate School of Journalism and has an MBA from Kellogg at Northwestern University. He and his wife, Sara Guralnick, a jewelry designer and children's book author, live in Chicago.

Acknowledgements

This book is lovingly dedicated to the memory of my parents, Norman and Phyllis Dubin, who gave me the gifts of love and laughter, taught me kindness and generosity, and all with a sense of humor.

. . . And to my dear wife, Sara Guralnick, who is the inspiration for all my creative endeavors.

Table of Contents

Introduction

"Norman doesn't follow the beat of a different drummer.
He follows the different beat of a whole marching band."
-Carl, his condo neighbor

Introduction

"It was hard work raising my parents.
In the end, they turned out alright."
-Joel

Norman seemed to know everybody in Chicago, and everybody in Chicago seemed to know Norman. Wherever Norman went, people came up to him. If someone approached him, who he didn't recognize, which wasn't often, he said he was a bank robber. He told them he didn't work on Wednesdays, of course, the day banks used to be closed many years ago.

The rare moments when nobody came up to Norman, he would look for – and usually find – someone he knew, even if he hadn't seen them in years or the connection was remote, maybe even less than a casual acquaintance. Strangers were fair game when the people well ran dry. If he couldn't find a friend, he would make one.

Norman was known at every high-end – and some not so high-end – restaurant in Chicago. Restaurants were one of his favorite stomping grounds. He was the man about town, the private ambassador for the hometown of his birth, his first love and where he spent his whole life. During his lifetime, he traveled around the US and even to Canada and Europe a few times but rarely strayed far from home. He wasn't much of a traveler or explorer, unless it was some new place in Chicago.

Then there was his wife, Phyllis. Together they were the uncrowned royalty of the Chicago restaurant scene. They were the couple everybody knew, even if Norman was the real star of the show, The Norman and Phyllis Show, that is.

At one restaurant, Norman's large tips earned him the honor of being inducted into The Golden Tipper's Club. His picture was on a wall there covered with photos of visiting Hollywood celebrities. The photo is barely noticeable among the wallpaper of the rich and famous. It didn't matter. They weren't regulars, like Norman. They were just interlopers, not real Chicagoans, nor, of course, as well-known around town as Norman.

At another restaurant, Norman was known as El Presidente by all the Mexican waiters. He didn't have to tell them his order. They already knew his favorite drink – Kettle One with a twist of lime – and entrée – Chicken Vesuvio – before he even sat down. His drink and meal just showed up at the table. The tip, as always, of course, was generous. Nothing less from El Presidente. He always came through for his people.

El Presidente had his own patronage army of Mexican waiters around Chicago. They even suggested he run for mayor. He would carry their vote, they assured him.

At Chicago's premiere deli, Manny's, Norman was a regular. He went there daily for lunch. If he didn't show up one day, they would call him to check in. They couldn't imagine Norman forgetting his daily lunch appointment. Manny's without Norman at the lunch table was unthinkable.

At the East Bank Club, Chicago's premiere health club and Norman's favorite hangout, and the hangout of famous Chicagoans he pestered, he was known as Stormin' Norman.

Norman and Phyllis were my parents, and they were, well, a bit nuts.

Norman has been gone over a decade. Since then, I've had a chance to catch my breath and reflect about his life. He was the father who loved me more than I could imagine, he used to always tell me.

Phyllis has been gone five years. She was the smothering Jewish mother and Norman's partner in crime, the crime of driving people, including me, crazy in public and at restaurants and beyond.

I still think about them every day.

Introduction

Growing up, I was Norman's shadow, his best friend, the pal who ran around Chicago with him. We were inseparable. Along the way, I heard every one of his cornball jokes, off-the-wall comments, and pithy wisdom – repeatedly. He loved to repeat himself. I guess, he thought I didn't get every saying and story the first time.

Growing up, I thought, if insanity is hereditary, I'm in big trouble.

Looking back, maybe Norman wasn't so crazy, after all. Behind his comic veneer was a devoted parent, a guide and mentor, and a serious businessman. He was the best life coach I could have ever had.

Norman supported every one of my hairbrained projects and then bragged about my achievements, or awards, to all his friends. He was my biggest promoter. He would always tell everybody again and again, "My kid did" such-and-such.

That was me, sometimes just "that kid."

Norman gave me the gift of a sense of humor. He taught me the secret of dealing with people – keep them laughing and, equally important, never take yourself too seriously.

Introduction

And Norman kept them laughing. He was a master at saying the wrong thing to the wrong person at the wrong time.

Phyllis taught me the art of interrogation, how to answer a stupid question with a stupid answer, but in a charming way—maybe not exactly charming – but with a dash of humor. She might have yelled but she quickly smiled and laughed afterwards.

Norman was fearless. He would approach anybody in his path and start talking. He bonded with the powerless and the powerful, whether a panhandler, someone waiting in line, a presidential candidate, a big-league football coach, or a politician.

Norman once asked a panhandler on the street why he just didn't get a job. At Manny's deli, he told Barack Obama he had seen him naked in the locker room at the East Bank Club. At another restaurant, he went up to former Chicago Bears coach Mike Ditka, the 1985 Superbowl champ, and snapped his picture and started chatting. They became fast friends.

He ran into the State's Attorney and the Secretary of State at other restaurants where Norman held court. He couldn't resist telling them how well they were running the State of Illinois. They were speechless, their look deadpan, probably giving him silent approval for his performance review of their jobs, as they quietly, and quickly, walked away.

If somebody had a title, Norman had to address them in public by their title, not their name. Norman's favorite was "doctor." "How are you today, doctor?" Norman used to say. A professor was called "professor," and a lawyer was called "attorney" or, "judge," if they were a judge, of course. Everybody else, mere mortals, were simply referred to by just their first name.

When Norman ran into his eye doctor on the street, he wouldn't look him directly in the eye. He would grope with his hands away from the doctor, as if he couldn't see him. "Doctor," Norman said, "Those contact lenses are great. I see just fine." The doctor, quiet and shy, politely chuckled and walked away.

The Norman and Phyllis Show

When he was out with Phyllis, together, they were two sticks of dynamite going off at the same time.

Some families have communication problems. Not Norman and Phyllis. They overcommunicated. Ask them anything. They would be happy to share or, more likely, overshare. They had to comment on everything. It was The Norman and Phyllis Show, the wackiest show never to appear on TV.

Nothing was taboo. Nothing was too intimate. Phyllis openly talked about her bodily functions and Norman always had some off-the-wall off-color comment.

I always thought, growing up, the job of parents was to embarrass their children in public.

I had a tough time raising my parents, but, in the end, I think they turned out alright.

Norman in the Bathroom with the Door Open

Norman was totally uninhibited. My wife, Sara, and I were visiting Norman and Phyllis at their condo. When we came in, Norman was standing in the bathroom with the door wide open, wearing only his bikini skivvies. He was pissing, his back to the door, a backhanded wave at us with his one free hand. Phyllis was in another room puttering around. She didn't even notice and didn't even care.

"Hi, Sara," he greeted us, as if there wasn't anything unusual about peeing nearly naked at home in front of guests. She covered her eyes and ran to the living room. She mumbled something unintelligible under her breath. For a minute, I thought she was going to shriek.

Norman came from Russian Jewish stock, among the first wave of Jewish immigrants from Russia in the late Nineteenth Century. He was proud of his roots and proud of our family's Chicago legacy. Of course, he also had to tell everybody.

Norman told everybody, pointing at me, "That kid is a fifth generation Chicagoan." That was usually followed by his rendition of "And, I'm a *Galitzianer* too," another Jewish tribe from Eastern Europe, unknown outside of his circle of friends of Eastern European Jewish descent.

Norman's life can be roughly divided into two phases – Aggravation Part One and Aggravation Part Two. Part One was his overbearing and smothering mother and grandmother, who raised him and nagged him senseless and who then, in Part Two, handed him over to his wife to finish the job, screaming him into submission.

Phyllis, the lion tamer, kept Norman in check with her ever-present battle cry, "Shut up Norman!"

Norman was raised without his father. His mother and grandmother kept him trapped at home. While incarcerated, they tightly restricted his visitors and playmates. Humor was his only escape.

Introduction

Norman had a few friends, who were neighbors, and an aunt and cousins who lived nearby. When he grew up and left the house, he made love to the world. He couldn't make enough friends. His desire to meet people was insatiable.

Then came Phyllis in her beehive hairdo, the mother of all Jewish mothers. Neurotic and hysterical, she screamed at Norman constantly about everything. No infraction, imagined or real, was too small. I was convinced as a kid, she communicated only by screaming and yelling. It was her normal tone of voice. It was just how she spoke.

Norman fought back with humor. He would parry and thrust with some joke or wise crack. When that didn't work, he just sat somewhere in the house, his nose stuck in The Wall Street Journal, and ignored her.

In public, they were the perfect couple, charming to a fault everywhere they went, whether at a restaurant, an event or just with friends. Phyllis's screaming and yelling carried her through the brief moments of calm she had to endure in public. She managed to hold it in. It wasn't easy.

Ultimately, it didn't matter. Nobody paid attention to Phyllis. Norman was the star of the show, the center of attention. Norman's charisma overcame all.

Norman's mother lived to one hundred, outliving three husbands and still getting speeding tickets well into her 90s. The two phases of aggravation of his life overlapped. Norman still had to contend with his out-of-control mother until long after he had married Phyllis. He had to deal with his mother even while she was sequestered in a nursing home to keep her from staging an elder coup d'etat to overthrow the place.

With this background, the roots of madness were obvious.

Norman loved the city. He loved the sights (especially the young women), the sounds, the crowds, the restaurants and their food, the street fairs, and the action. The restaurants were key. Phyllis's bad cooking nearly killed him. He needed a culinary outlet. Otherwise, he might have starved.

Norman made the ultimate sacrifice for me. He moved to the suburbs. He and Phyllis moved out of the city shortly after they got married. They were part of the Great White Flight after the Second World War. They came in anticipation of my arrival, looking for more living space and better schools – not for the lawns.

Introduction

Norman hated every minute of it. He wasn't a homeowner and wasn't handy or a fan of doing things around the house. He was at war with the lawn. He let the weeds take over until the neighbors complained. He ran back into the city, with me in tow, whenever he could.

Norman would use any excuse – a new restaurant, a grand opening of some store, an exhibit at a gallery or museum, a street fair, an art fair, anything – just to get out of the house and go to the city. "Let's shoot over to . . .," or "Let's see this new . . .," he would always say. He carried a list of places to visit in his pocket, ready to unsheathe at any moment.

Once I was out of the house, the studio for The Norman and Phyllis Show relocated to a condo on Chicago's lakefront. They sold the house in Skokie in less than a year, and its overgrown lawn, and finally moved back to their beloved city. They couldn't get back fast enough.

Words weren't Norman's friends. He wasn't a great orator. He often got tongue-tied saying the simplest things. He sometimes just couldn't put a sentence together. Sometimes, he just made words up. Yet, people somehow understood him. He always got his point across. They still loved him. His humor, yet again, always carried him through.

Norman had the gift of gab. He could talk his way into anything. He never ran for office – he hated politics – and he wasn't a celebrity. He wasn't an entertainer either, but he knew how to entertain – a joke here, a funny story there, and Norman could break the ice.

Norman could open doors. He had the thickest Rolodex from years of schmoozing and socializing on the street and at restaurants. He had a network second to none around Chicago. Norman had connections everywhere for everything.

"I have a guy," Norman always used to say.

The closest Norman ever came to any real political power was when he was appointed by Mayor Richard M. Daley to help the Mayor's Committee on Special Events. I'll never know how he got to the mayor. I can only imagine it was through some back door, a friend of a friend of a friend who knew someone in the mayor's office.

It might have been the CD Norman sent to Daley of the song The Little Tin Box from the musical, Fiorello. The song is about corrupt politicians in New York in the 1920s testifying to a judge how they paid for their extravagances by saving money in a tin box. The mayor sent Norman a cordial letter thanking him for his thoughtfulness.

Introduction

Maybe it was just Norman's way of buttering up the mayor, implying that Daley was Chicago's Fiorello. Just as Fiorello La Guardia battled New York's corrupt Tammany Hall, to Norman, Daley was Chicago's savior from its infamous corrupt past.

Norman was a networker. He understood soft power. It was a skill he inherited from his wheeler dealer Grandpa Ike, who arrived in Chicago as a penniless immigrant in the 1880s and, starting with a pushcart, ended up owning an enormously successful cap business, mostly through making connections.

Norman gave me the gift of gab and, with it, his ability to build and maintain and nourish relationships. He taught me how to be a people person.

Norman's other base of power, besides his favorite restaurants, was the East Bank Club. He knew how to work the locker room, the racquetball court and, of course, the bar. He knew every inch of the club and its best meeting spots.

It was also Norman's favorite spot for his other pastime, girl watching. Norman had an eye for the ladies. He had to make a comment about every passing babe. His comments ranged from the inappropriate to the lewd. He even was, at times, an unrepentant flirt.

Norman's wandering eye followed the parade of eye candy around town right to the tight leotards at the East Bank Club. I often wondered if he had a squeeze on the side. I didn't have to ask. He told me before I even had the chance.

Norman complained he couldn't have a mistress, since everybody in town knew him. He just couldn't keep it a secret.

In the end, it was all just talk. It was just another of Norman's tall tales to charm people. He was completely devoted and faithful to Phyllis to the very end.

Norman the Jewish guy grew up in an era when Jews lived and worked together, whether by choice or by circumstance. He naturally thought, "Isn't everybody Jewish?"

Norman still encountered antisemitism, especially rampant in the workplace and in housing – a Jew just couldn't live or work anywhere – as he was growing up. As with every other challenge in life, he overcame it with his characteristic sense of humor.

Introduction

Norman once told a Catholic priest that he didn't eat meat on Fridays either, just in case "one of us is wrong." His other pet project was to teach Yiddish to every Mexican waiter in Chicago. One of his favorite greetings was *"zei gezunt,"* or "go in health," his way of saying goodbye.

Norman could be incredibly generous. He brought food regularly to a housebound paraplegic friend. He and Phyllis once gave a waitress a ride home to a distant suburb, when she missed her train after work.

When I was out of town on business, Norman and Phyllis insisted on taking Sara to dinner, so she wouldn't be home alone. He would pick her up at our house and bring her back home afterward and wouldn't take no for an answer.

Norman's Infamous Soggy Cigar Stub in a Baggie

When it wasn't in his mouth, Norman carried around a chewed-up cigar in a small plastic baggie.

"I don't really smoke it," Norman used to say. "I only chew on it."

It was pretty gross. It was wet and soggy and oozed a brown liquid. The top was chewed into a flat disk. It looked like a lollipop made of tobacco.

When Norman wore a tan trench coat in the fall and spring, with his short curly hair and cigar stub in hand, he looked a little like Columbo, the iconic detective from the 70s TV series. He even talked like Columbo too in chopped up half sentences.

Norman and Phyllis's world is a blend of both Chicago and Jewish history. It starts when Norman's ancestors arrived in Chicago from Russia in the late Nineteenth Century, and Phyllis's two decades later, and continues with the saga of an immigrant Jewish family in America over the next century and a half.

Norman and Phyllis's story is the colorful intersection of those two worlds.

Norman and Phyllis were a Chicago legend, at least, in their own mind.

This is their story. The story of The Norman and Phyllis Show.

It starts, where they were always the guest of honor, at their favorite restaurants.

The Golden Tipper's Club

"You can't eat at Manny's every day!"
-Norman's doctor

"Are you a bank teller? I'm a bank robber.
You must have seen me at your bank."
-Norman, when someone recognized him

Norman loved to meet people. He loved to see and be seen. He loved to be out in public. He loved to mingle. He would talk to anybody. Anybody, at least, who would listen.

And, to Norman, the best place to hunt his prey was restaurants. Not just any restaurant. It had to be a restaurant where he knew – or thought he knew – someone. If he didn't know anyone, it didn't matter. He would meet someone new. New people were always welcome in Norman's world.

It didn't always have to be a top-tier restaurant – though some of Chicago's best known: Gibsons, Gene & Georgetti, Carmine's and Tuscany – were on his regular rotation. Step aside Michelin Guide. In Chicago, it was Norman's List. He was the authoritative source. If Norman liked it, and Michelin didn't, Norman overruled.

Michelin was an outsider. Not Norman. He was the authentic insider, the true local yokel, the consummate Chicago native (four generations deep, he told everyone). He owned Chicago's restaurant scene.

Norman's List was the guide to Chicago's best dining or, at least, its best celebrity hunting grounds. Michelin might have had its expert scouts. Norman's review team, consisting, of course, of only Norman, unpolished and unprofessional compared to Michelin, had a personal touch Michelin lacked.

Norman's List was never written down. It was all in Norman's head, part of the Legend of Norman's great oral tradition. Just ask Norman, he would tell you his restaurant pick of the day. His list of famous restaurants was legendary – like Norman himself – in his own mind. It was always changing, week to week, day to day. New restaurants were always being added, while old ones were always being removed.

Norman's other source for new restaurants were his buddies at the East Bank Club. The East Bank Club was a celebrity destination itself complete with high-end restaurants and bars on each floor. It was just the kind of watering hole Norman craved. It always buzzed with interesting people.

Norman, of course, was one of its founding members, when it opened in 1980. He knew people at other health clubs who moved over to the then new East Bank Club. He was part of the trailblazing crowd. He had to make the move. It was a natural fit for the man-about-town.

The East Bank Club was Norman's second home and played a big part in his life. The restaurant suggestions from the East Bank Club mavens were hit and miss. Some were winners, others phenomenal flops, especially if they had "Fusion" in the name, which Norman didn't care for.

Norman once took us to a so-called fusion restaurant on Clark Street in Lincoln Park on the suggestion of one of his East Bank buddies. The food was terrible – Norman called it Martian food – and Phyllis screamed at Norman. We ate, what was edible, and left and Norman never mentioned the restaurant again.

Every new restaurant still had the potential to be a gold mine of new friends or, better yet, long lost old friends. So, Norman had to check out each one personally.

Norman preferred restaurants where he could mingle with celebrities, politicians, businesspeople, and power brokers. If not a power broker, Norman would settle for a not-so-powerful old chum from the past. In fact, he would settle for just about anybody. With Norman, it didn't matter, as long as they were living and breathing and willing to chat.

Food was secondary. The potential to meet people was more important. The purpose of a restaurant wasn't to eat. It was to meet people, according to Norman. Restaurants were also the weekend refuge from the ravages of Phyllis's non-cooking during the week. Even a bad meal at a restaurant was better than her inedible homemade meal.

Norman loved a home cooked meal, as long as it was cooked in somebody's else home or, even better, in a restaurant.

If he didn't see anybody he knew, or who was worth knowing, he would get up from the table and stand in the middle of the restaurant. He would rotate around like a lighthouse beacon, looking for someone, anyone, he might know, even distantly.

Norman liked to be the first to break the ice.

"Hey, did you go to Senn?" Norman went to Senn High School in the 1940s. It was Norman's starting point with strangers he recognized, or thought he recognized, from high school. Half the time, they had no idea who he was. Nobody was ever unfriendly or hostile. People were always cordial, if a bit mystified by a stranger approaching them with such an odd question.

If that didn't work, he would go back further. "I knew you at Goudy or Trumbull, right?" Those were the two elementary schools he attended in the 30s and 40s. Memories that far back were hazier, ending up in more deadpan stares.

Norman was fearless. He just shrugged it off. Maybe next time he would hit pay dirt, Norman thought.

When someone, who Norman didn't know, recognized him first, he would say, "Are you a bank teller? I'm a bank robber. You must have seen me at your bank." Then he would add this disclaimer. "I don't work on Wednesdays," a reference to a practice decades ago when banks were closed on Wednesdays.

Sometimes, he would add, "Maybe you saw my picture in the post office," another reference to ancient times before the Internet, when mugshots of wanted fugitives were on post office walls.

"You remember me," Norman's other line, when all else failed, "I was the guy with the big nose and floppy ears."

If the people well ran dry, at least, there was always people watching. All of Norman's favorite restaurants were in busy locations with a lot of foot traffic. Inevitably, some strange person, or more likely, and more important to Norman, some hot babe would pass by. Norman just had to comment, sometimes within earshot of the person. He couldn't help himself. It was Norman being Norman again, saying the wrong thing to the wrong person at the wrong time.

Norman's Waiters: The Privileged Few

Norman had high standards for the privileged few waiters who wanted to serve him.

He told every waiter lucky enough to serve him, "You will be rewarded," Norman-speak for a generous tip. Norman had a reputation around town for being a big tipper.

To earn their keep, the waiter had to follow Norman's two rules.

First, don't upstage Norman. Second, don't be late.

The waiter couldn't tell any jokes, or say anything else, for that matter, to take attention away from the guest of honor – Norman. Norman would tell any waiter who attempted to make a joke, "Me comedian. You waiter." Norman had to be the center of attention. Norman's waiters were expected to laugh – or pretend to laugh – at all his jokes, corny or not.

Norman would sometimes bend this rule for a waiter he thought was colorful or had funny stories or advice. He even tolerated obnoxious waiters now and then, if they followed Norman's second rule – food must be brought within a reasonable amount of time.

Norman's second rule: don't be late. If a waiter disappeared for a long time – even if for a valid reason, like the kitchen being backed up – Norman would ask the waiter, when he returned, "How was your vacation?"

An exhaustive list of every restaurant Norman touched could fill another book. Basically, he held court at three main restaurants. Manny's Cafeteria & Delicatessen, his daily lunch staple, with Gibsons Bar & Steakhouse and Gene & Georgetti reserved for the weekends. Norman's power base rested with these three restaurants and, the fourth, his second home, the East Bank Club.

Looking for Norman? Go to one of these hotspots. That is where you would find him.

Norman also hosted people at his restaurants. They could be his office coworkers or business acquaintance for lunch, friends or family from out of town for dinner, or even a spur-of-the-moment snack with anybody, any time of day.

Everybody knew Norman could be counted on for his hospitality and generosity. He was only a phone call, or an email, away. He rarely said no.

Norman always had to pay. When one of Norman's friends threw him a birthday party at Carnivale, a restaurant in Fulton Market, they preempted Norman by gathering everybody's credit cards at the door. Norman didn't know what to do when he held up his credit card in the air and waved it around, and the waiter ignored him.

When Norman did pay, he wasn't afraid to go large. Phyllis insisted, despite my objections, on throwing an expensive party for my fiftieth birthday at the East Bank Club. Norman went along and footed the bill. In addition, Sara hired a piano player, a Jewish singer, and an authentic Middle Eastern belly dancer. She put together a world map with pins in every country I had visited and decorated the tables with party favors, fancy napkin holders, and placemats with bits of trivia about me.

The Mayor of Manny's:
The Daily Lunch Destination

If the National Register of Historic Places ever listed Norman's hangouts, Manny's Deli would be on the top of the list. In a decades-long ritual, Norman went to Manny's every day. It was located on

Jefferson Street just north of Roosevelt Road. Everybody knew when Norman was there. MAZLTOV was in the parking lot. He didn't have a reserved spot, but when the space was available, he liked to park by the chain-link fence at the entrance.

Manny's was Chicago's most famous Jewish deli, often portrayed in the Chicago media.

And Norman was dubbed The Mayor of Manny's by his lunch buddies.

When Norman didn't show up for lunch, Kenny Raskin, the owner of Manny's, would say he had to call Norman's home to check in. Manny's wouldn't be the same without its honorary ambassador.

Manny's was a cafeteria with a complete array of food, both Jewish and not. The typical Jewish fare included corned beef and roast beef with delicious potato pancakes and the obligatory matzo ball soup. There was whitefish and lox (a must have at any Jewish deli), and brisket alongside spaghetti, beef stew and chopped liver and sides of potatoes and coleslaw. Mile-high pastrami sandwiches could be on onion rolls or, of course, the ultimate in Jewish dining – rye bread.

Nobody ever left Manny's hungry. Portions were large and hearty, even if they made Norman's doctor cringe. "You can't eat at Manny's every day," she used to tell Norman.

Plates overfilled with food were slid across the counter for customers to put on their trays. The line for lunch was always long, sometimes even out the door. Manny's was just south of downtown Chicago off a busy retail shopping area on Roosevelt Road and east of the University of Illinois Chicago (UIC), nicknamed "Circle" from its former name as UIC Circle after the circular plaza in the middle of the campus.

Behind the counter, Gene juggled knives like a pro as he cut sandwiches for Norman. Gene and Norman always chatted about the day's events as they passed each other in line. Gene himself was a local celebrity, appearing with his bushy mustache in photos of Manny's lunch counter in Chicago newspaper articles, many framed on a wall near the cash register.

Norman went to Manny's because of the food and, of course, like all his other restaurants, the customers. It may have only been a coincidence, but in an odd way, he was returning to his roots. His immigrant ancestors settled on Roosevelt Road when they arrived from Russia after a stint in Atlanta in the 1880s.

In the late Nineteenth Century, Roosevelt Road was Chicago's immigrant gateway. Jewish, Italian, and Irish immigrants rubbed elbows on the streets crowded as much with people as with horses and pushcarts. Norman's grandfather ran one of those pushcarts, losing a leg after it rolled over, nearly crushing him.

Maxwell Street around the corner was the city's famous open-air market until it was closed in the 1990s and redeveloped for homes and expansion of Circle campus.

By Norman's time, Maxwell Street was already in decline, and the immigrants had moved on. A smattering of small clothing stores remained, some owned by descendants of the original Jewish immigrants. The rest of the old shops had been replaced by retail stores, some small, some chains, the population reflective of the current residents, Whites, Blacks and Latinos from the surrounding neighborhoods to the south and west of Roosevelt Road.

The area during the Norman era was still busy and packed with people, many from the army of downtown office workers, descending each day on Manny's for lunch.

Manny's was also a pitstop for city officials and local business leaders. Cops always stopped by to take a seat and grab a bite. Many politicians made pit stops there, including Barack Obama before he was president. Rumor has it the corned beef and cherry pie were his favorites.

The list of people Norman ran into at Manny's over the years was endless. He never went there without knowing someone. It started as soon as he walked in the door. "Hey, Norman," someone would wave, waiting in line tray in hand.

He once ran into David Axelrod, Obama's former senior advisor and later a CNN commentator, sitting quietly by himself at a corner table eating lunch. Of course, Norman had to go over and introduce himself. "That's David Axelrod over there," Norman said to me. "I'm going to say hi."

Axelrod was a national personality but not a celebrity people normally pestered in public – except for Norman.

Axelrod was polite but reserved, not sure how to react to this overly friendly stranger. Axelrod finished eating and smiled at Norman as left the restaurant.

But it was the fateful day Norman met Axelrod's onetime boss, Obama, face-to-face at Manny's when the course of history changed for me personally. Norman harmlessly and humorously embarrassed me in a way only an eccentric father could do to a son.

On the other hand, Norman considered dinners on the weekend a family affair. I knew whenever he called, especially on a Saturday or Sunday, it was for dinner. He always started the conversation the same, "I don't want to be possessive, but . . ." My wife and I often wondered if, when the weekend arrived, he just couldn't stand to be alone with Phyllis.

Norman always preferred to eat out. When that didn't work out, he ordered in, and we ate at the condo. Norman's favorites were the staple of the non-Kosher Jewish diet: ribs or Chinese. Phyllis always called all Chinese food "chop suey," even when she ordered something else. When she said, "Let's have chop suey," I knew she really meant Chinese food.

Occasionally, Norman took us out for Chinese. We went to his favorite restaurant in Chinatown, Evergreen Restaurant on Wentworth Avenue. On Christmas, a holiday many Jews celebrate in Chinatown, we would go with a group of Jewish friends to Phoenix Restaurant on Archer. Of course, since many Jews went to Chinese restaurants, Norman would still always run into people he knew even there.

If, by chance, we ended up going out twice in a day, say, for both lunch and dinner, Norman used to say between meals, "When is the next feeding time?"

Gene & Georgetti: "El Presidente"

Saturday nights were reserved for Gene & Georgetti, a small Italian steakhouse in River North on Franklin Street next to the L tracks. Gene & Georgetti opened during the Second World War and has been ranked among the country's top 50 steakhouses ever since. It was also on the go-to list of a few Hollywood celebrities passing through town.

Norman once spotted Vince Vaughn passing by the bar, but the restaurant was so crowded he couldn't get close enough to talk to him or even shake his hand. Vaughn stood out, not because of his fame, but because he was at least a foot taller than everybody else in line. He squeezed his shoulders, sandwiched between the people sitting and standing by the bar and those seated at the tables close by.

Like any typical Saturday night, the narrow path between the bar and the tables up front was full of hungry customers either waiting, or on their way, to be seated. Sometimes the crowd pressed right up against the door.

Norman and Phyllis started going to Gene &
Georgetti since the beginning of time, or at least,
since my childhood.

It wasn't fancy. From the outside, it looked like an
unassuming apartment building on a corner under
the train tracks. Inside, tables were next to each
other, almost touching, from the main dining room
right up to the bar. The simple white table clothes
gave it a chummy feel more reminiscent of a
neighborhood joint, or maybe the dining room of
an Italian home, than a nationally known stomping
ground for celebrities.

It was just Norman's kind of place – overcrowded,
noisy and intimate. If he didn't see anyone he
knew coming in, he would be going out. With
tables on top of each other, it was impossible not
to hear a neighbor's conversation or, at least,
accidentally rub elbows.

Norman's ears were always perked. The main
dining room, where Norman's table was always
reserved, was so small, Norman could even hear
conversations across the room. They bounced from
walls painted in Italian Renaissance style back to
Norman's lap.

A young man once proposed to a woman at a table
in the corner. They tried to be discreet. But privacy

wasn't on Gene & Georgetti's long menu. Everybody in the restaurant overheard and heartily cheered and clapped.

Norman wanted to go over and tell the future husband there was still time to reconsider. I discouraged him. I sometimes had to be the adult when out with Norman.

Three of the Mexican waiters honored Norman with the title "El Presidente." Two were named Jose and another named Juan. They all came from the same small town in rural Mexico, where they told us, everybody knew everybody. The crowd on Saturday night, where the regulars all knew each other, reminded them of their hometown.

Norman's favorite dish was the Chicken Vesuvio, large enough to split with the table, like the huge salad and basket of bread. Phyllis always ordered the white fish, her favorite, wherever she could get it, and Gene & Georgetti always had it. They also liked the eggplant parmesan and the huge pieces of ravioli.

Out of stock? Maybe for some other patron. Never for El Presidente. Tiny as its kitchen was, Gene & Georgetti always delivered what Norman wanted.

All the waiters knew Norman's favorite drink: Kettle One. He never had to order it. It just showed up at his table, as soon as he sat down.

El Presidente tipped well. He once slipped a few bucks in the pocket of a waiter who picked up his napkin on the floor. The waiter said to me in Spanish, *"Sin El Presidente, no hay restaurante. (Without El Presidente, there is no restaurant.)"*

I spoke only Spanish with the waiters. Norman was impressed with my fluency but still always said, "I swear I picked up the wrong kid in the hospital."

Sometimes Norman drifted off to go people hunting at other tables. I once said to the waiter, *"Nos abandonó para otro amante. (He left us for another lover.),"* and he laughed. He knew. He understood Norman as much as we did.

Not to be outdone, Norman had to use the few – and it was very few – words he knew of Spanish. When he had leftovers, he would ask in a solidly gringo accent for a *"bolsa de perro,"* the literal translation for "doggy bag," which made no sense in Spanish. Of course, they all understood he meant a *"bolsa para llevar,"* the correct term in Spanish for a bag for leftovers.

Done eating, Norman worked his way through the crowds out the door, chatting with everyone he knew, which was just about everybody. Leaving Gene & Georgetti on a Saturday night for Norman was as challenging as getting through the front door. It could take him another half hour just to wade through the crowd, saying hello to everyone.

Out the door, his beloved MAZELTOV was waiting. Rich, the valet guy, or his son, also a valet, leaned against the open door, waiting for Norman's arrival. Somehow, somebody had already telegraphed the valet – El President was on his way.

Next Stop, Gibsons: The Golden Tippers Club

Not exhausted from his Saturday night excursion to Gene & Georgetti, Norman was ready for action again on Sunday night at Gibsons. Also a top Chicago steakhouse, Gibsons was on Rush Street. Unlike Gene & Georgetti, which was in a desolate corner of River North with no foot traffic outside, Gibsons was in the heart of the city's busiest restaurant and night club district.

Norman and Phyllis were regulars at Gibsons since it opened in 1989. It was more than a dining experience. It was the ultimate people watching destination, and Norman was the ultimate people watcher. With its prime Rush Street location, it couldn't be anything less.

Gibsons was busy every day of the week. Weekends were no different. Without a reservation, the wait could be over an hour. Not for Norman. He knew the owner, Steve Lombardo, and the maître d', Kathy. He had a marker. He could come whenever he wanted.

Besides Steve and Kathy, the rest of the staff at Gibsons knew Norman. Like every other restaurant he touched, Norman ingratiated himself with everybody, from the Assyrian and Slovakian valets at the front door, who parked his MAZLVTOV, to the waiters and kitchen staff in the back. When Norman wanted an odd substitution not on the menu, he got it. Anything for Norman.

Norman's secret was his big – and open – wallet. He was a card-carrying member of The Golden Tipper's Club. Norman was so anointed by a waiter who once served Warren Buffett during a visit to Chicago. Buffett allegedly tipped the waiter a couple of hundred dollars. The waiter founded the big tipper club in his honor.

Norman heard the story later from the waiter. Norman never actually met Buffett, and the fictional club, of course, was founded only by the waiter. Still, Norman was thrilled to be a member of the same hallowed club as a business giant like Buffett. Maybe not hundreds of dollars, but Norman tipped well.

The walls of Gibson's lobby, where people waited shoulder to shoulder to be seated, were plastered with photos, many signed, of athletes, Hollywood personalities, newscasters, and other celebrities. Above the coat check area, there was a photo of Norman in a suit and tie, his arm around an equally well-dressed Phyllis, both smiling. It was easy to miss among the mass of pictures of famous people. How it got there, or who put it there, was anybody's guess.

But the coat check lady, Peaches, knew the photo. She could always pick out Norman's picture above her head. Norletta Knighton, her real name, was Gibson's den mother. She knew the name of every regular, celebrity or not, including Norman. When Norman and Phyllis came, she always came out from behind the counter and gave them a big hug. She treated everyone, even us, like family.

When not working at Gibsons, Peaches was a singer and gave us CDs of her performances. She also made sure, whenever we ordered carry out, with or without Norman, our orders were on time and complete.

Norman sometimes brought large parties to Gibsons. Getting a table was never a problem, except once – when the Chicago Bears football team showed up after a big game one Sunday evening. Like anything Chicago, Norman loved the Bears, even when they disappointed, as they often did. He bowed to celebrities greater them himself – he had no choice – when they took over his reserved table.

Norman just looked on quietly and waited patiently for the big table to open. One of the Bears came up to Norman afterward and thanked him personally for being so gracious.

The Bears were sacred to Norman. They were his personal team, nobody else's. Even when the Bears weren't there, Norman used to sneak into the bar during their game to take a quick peak at the score.

Their former coach, Mike Ditka, famous for taking them to victory in the 1985 Super Bowl, was also a Gibsons regular. Norman spotted him once as he was about to go in. Norman quickly pulled out his camera and took a picture of Ditka along a wall outside the restaurant.

Fortunately, Norman got a good clean head shot of Ditka centered right in the middle of the frame. He had finally learned how to use the camera. Until then, he had an album full of foreheads, cheeks and chins.

When Norman took pictures of people, he told them to "Say Shit," instead of "Cheese," or "Smile."

In a rare moment of common sense, thank God, he didn't tell Ditka to say shit.

After that, whenever Ditka saw Norman at Gibson's, he would smile and give him a warm handshake.

Gibsons was a traditional steakhouse, and Norman loved their London broil, and Phyllis the white fish. No vegetarian meals for Norman. "I didn't come here for the fruit plate," he used to say.

He sometimes would pick food from other people's plates without asking. If he saw a tasty dish, he had to try himself, his excuse was "I'm saving a life," claiming it was unhealthy for them, but not for Norman, of course.

This must be either genetic, or a family tradition, because eating off other's plates, according to my wife, is a habit I've also picked up.

Norman's favorite waiter was Sheldon. Except for being Black, Sheldon was about my height and build. We both had short hair and glasses and a welcoming smile. There was some resemblance. Norman used to always say, "That's your half-brother over there." Sheldon always got a kick whenever he heard that.

The Viagra Triangle and Carmine's

Across the street from Gibsons to the north was a small triangular park. Bounded by Rush and State Streets and Bellevue Place, Mariano Park was visible from Gibsons and the surrounding restaurants. It was the best open-air theater in town.

People walked dogs, couples strolled together and young girls paraded by. It was the old farts ogling the girls, some suggestively dressed during Chicago's hot summers, that gave the park its infamous nickname of The Viagra Triangle. Norman could be counted among those old farts, making inappropriate comments under his breath when a hot chic passed by.

Facing The Viagra Triangle, across from Rush Street, was another of Norman's occasional favorite haunts, Carmine's. Gibsons had a ribbon of tables outside, which Norman loved when available. Carmine's, expansive outdoor seating had the feel of a European café and was where Norman would go for a change of pace during Chicago's notoriously hot summers.

Carmine's was an Italian restaurant with a wide menu. It was also a ringside seat overlooking The Viagra Triangle. It had indoor seating, but the tables outside were the most coveted. They had the best access to the stream of people walking by on the street.

Norman, of course, had an inside guy. Not surprisingly, he knew the maître d'. Glen was a young tall thin guy with glasses. He was half Jewish, half Italian, and wore two neckties at the same time. He made sure Norman got his VIP booth outside.

When Norman saw someone he knew pass by, which happened almost every time, he would invite them to sit down at the table, order them a drink, or even a meal. "Pull up a seat," he said. "We have room."

Norman once recognized Jesse White, when he was the Illinois Secretary of State, leaving Carmine's after a meal. Norman had to go up to him and shake his hand. He told White he was doing a good job running the Department of Motor Vehicles, as if he needed Norman's approval. He thanked White for expediting his last drivers license renewal. White smiled and thanked Norman politely and then walked away.

Norman's Honorable Mentions

Though not as often as his three favorites, Norman frequented other famous Chicago restaurants.

Among the honorable mentions was Cannella's, another family-run Italian restaurant with a long history. Norman followed Cannella's for many years from its location on Lincoln Avenue, then Huron Street and finally on Grand Avenue, where it finally closed around 2005.

His favorite waiter was Mike, who was sarcastic and knew how to put Norman in his place – respectfully. "OK, what do you want already?" Mike would say with an attitude. Norman loved it. He laughed at his humorous put downs.

Nearby in Little Italy, Norman went occasionally to Tuscany's on Taylor Street. Don the waiter, famous throughout Chicago, knew how to kid around with Norman. Don called Norman "high maintenance." He said Phyllis was a saint for putting up with Norman. If Don only knew, it was the other way around. Phyllis was high maintenance, and Norman was the saint.

Down the street from Tuscany's was Tufano's Vernon Street tap, a family-run Italian bar and grill popular with the locals. The fried calamari and big bowl of roasted chicken were among Norman's favorites.

Even for breakfast, Norman had a favorite destination. He normally scarfed down toast and coffee at home before heading to the office, but occasionally would stop by Lou Mitchell's on Jackson Boulevard, usually before an early meeting.

Lou Mitchell's, like Manny's, was a center of power in Chicago. Strategically located just west of the Loop, it was popular with politicians, including Mayor Daley. Norman wasn't as well connected there, but he still liked the hubbub and the chance to run into people he knew.

Then There was the East Bank Club . . .

When Norman wasn't at the bar, he would grab a bite in one of the East Bank Club's restaurants. Sometimes on week nights, he would take us all to Maxwell's on the first floor, or The Grill on the second floor. Sometimes we also went there for lunch on Sunday.

The waiters and waitresses were mostly Mexican. Not just at the East Bank, but at all of Norman's restaurants, he loved Mexican wait staff. Besides tipping them well, his other mission was to teach them Yiddish or, at least, something close. When he was done eating, he would say, "*genug*," meaning "enough."

Norman didn't really speak Yiddish. He struggled with English, supposedly his native tongue, but like the descendants of many Jewish immigrants, who lost Yiddish after only one generation, he still knew many colorful words and sayings.

Norman knew enough, at least, to teach them greetings and a few basic phrases.

Some Mexican waiters suggested he should run for mayor. They said he would carry the vote of every Mexican waiter in Chicago.

If you ever go to a restaurant in Chicago, and a Mexican waiter or waitress greets you with *"Shalom Uvrachah,"* Norman has probably been there.

Norman Meets Obama

"I've seen you naked in the locker room at the East Bank Club."
-Norman told Obama

Norman Meets Obama

"And I'm a Republican too!"
-Norman told Obama at Manny's

I was on my way to lunch, walking leisurely down LaSalle Street, when Norman pulls up in MAZLTOV. He rolled down the window and yelled, "Hey, Obama is at Manny's." He came out of nowhere. I didn't see or hear him coming down the street. "C'mon, let's go meet Obama."

That was Stormin' Norman. He could come out of the dark at any time. I never knew when.

It was August 9, 2004 – an infamous day etched forever in my memory. Obama was running for the U.S. Senate and John Edwards for Vice President. They were at Manny's for a campaign whistle stop. It was a natural for Obama, a fellow Chicagoan who happened to also love Manny's.

Still a bit surprised, I jumped in the car. Traffic downtown was busy but still normal for a lunchtime on weekdays.

When we got to Manny's, Jefferson Street was a media and Secret Service fortress. Media vans with their antenna and equipment and black limos were parked up and down the street in both directions. Civilians couldn't get near the place. The street was effectively blocked out to the horizon.

The regular lunch crowd, the uninformed mere mortals, unlike Norman who seemed to always have the inside scoop on everything going on in Chicago, didn't know top brass was visiting. They stood in a line extending from the entrance down to Roosevelt Road and around the corner.

Getting into Manny's, for once, was formidable. Between the vehicles and the crowd and the traffic, it looked like our hero, Norman, might not conquer the palace either. For a minute, I too had my doubts. I was going to suggest we turn back. Norman was undeterred. The crowds and the media wouldn't stop him.

He had an idea.

The entrance to Manny's had two doors. The one on the right led to the cafeteria counter. The one on the left only opened out and was the exit from the dining area.

A guard stood in front of the exit door on the left. He was unmistakably Secret Service: an earpiece with a coiled cord, a dark suit and tie, and a crew cut.

Norman went up to the Secret Service guy at the door on the left. I obediently followed. Norman asked when we could go in. The Secret Service guy said, "after the press conference." Norman detected a Southern drawl. "Where are you from?" Norman asked. "Arkansas," he replied.

That was Norman's hook. Norman had cousins in Osceola, a tiny town in rural Arkansas. They were the only Jewish family in the town, owning a general store in the once picturesque downtown. Norman and Phyllis had visited them on their honeymoon, and my wife and I eventually also made the pilgrimage. We kept in touch over the years until one of them passed and the rest of the family moved away to Dallas.

So, there was Norman chatting up the Secret Service agent, telling him about our family in Osceola, as if they were best buds, maybe even homies, from the same town in the South.

Fortunately, Norman didn't bore the Secret Service guy with his bogus story about our Southern family in the Civil War. "We have relatives who fought on both sides of the Civil War," complete nonsense since our family arrived from Russia fifteen years after the Civil War ended.

For some kooky reason, Norman thought our Southern ancestors were Confederates. Maybe it was because the "relations," as the family in Osceola called themselves, had a small marble plaque on the shelf, saying *"Shalom Y'all"* to display their twin bona fides as both Southern and Jewish.

Then Norman noticed a little round badge on the Secret Service agent's lapel. It was color coded with some strange numbers and letters. What it meant was obviously classified. Norman knew better. But Norman being Norman, he had to ask. "What's that mean," he said, pointing at the pin. "I can't tell you that, Sir," the Secret Service agent said in an Arkansas drawl.

Suddenly, the press conference ended, and he let us in. Success. The exit door trick worked.

The dining room was still completely packed with media and Secret Service. There wasn't room to move. I had to elbow my way through the crowd. Norman followed close behind.

Then, there he was, in the flesh, Barack Obama, standing right in front of me. I couldn't believe I was lucky enough to get through the thicket.

He looked at me and warmly extended his hand. "What's your name, young man?" Of course, he didn't know I was five years older than him.

I told him my name, and then he looked at Norman. For a moment, I forgot Norman was still there. He had tagged along and was standing right behind me.

"You look familiar," Obama said to Norman.

Then it happened. My worst fear coming true, Norman saying something stupid and embarrassing me.

"Yeah, I've seen you naked in the locker room at the East Bank Club." Norman spoke naturally, even nonchalantly, as if they were old friends, just two guys chatting at neighboring lockers.

Obama politely chuckled. He didn't say a word. He didn't flinch. He was straight-faced. He didn't look or act shocked. What could he say? What could he do? How could he respond to something so outrageous?

Somehow Norman thought they had this special tie, maybe a kinship, maybe part of the same brotherhood or fraternity, because they were both members of the same elite health club.

Maybe Norman thought himself local royalty meeting national royalty – imagined greatness meeting true greatness. Sometimes, I just never could figure out what was in his head.

Then Norman went for the kill. I was already cringing. When I thought it couldn't get worse, it did.

"And I'm a Republican too!" Oh no, I thought, the end is near. The Secret Service is listening – and watching.

Obama raised his fists above his head and declared, "I love to enlighten Republicans."

Ready to take cover under the nearest table, I saw a Secret Service agent nervously glancing at us. He was taller than our friend from Arkansas. He had broad shoulders like a football player. He looked like an ex-linebacker. His muscles were about to burst out of his shirt. He looked ready to pounce.

It was, of course, all in my imagination, probably just my paranoia over Norman's craziness. I should have already been used to it. I still never knew what to expect most of the time.

Before it was too late, or before the Secret Service tackled us, I thought, I had to do damage control. I had to cut short Norman's brush with fame to keep us, but especially Norman and his mouth, out of trouble.

"Every family has got one," I said to Obama, as I gently pushed my father aside.

Norman Meets Obama

We then went over to see John Edwards, standing by himself nearby. He shook my hand and thanked me for coming in a booming voice. His language was canned and rehearsed. His smile seemed fake. He sounded like a typical politician, phony and insincere. There was nothing special about him. He wasn't charismatic, or personable, like Obama. The contrast was striking.

Norman didn't really know Edwards or have anything in common enough with him to approach him and cause more verbal damage. For once, it was a rare moment, when we were on safe ground.

Though our encounter was brief, Obama's sincerity and down-to-earth nature showed through. He seemed like just an ordinary guy, like someone you could go out with for a bite, or even a drink. He connected with people immediately on a personal level, with people as people, rather than as political objects whose votes were to be sought after.

Obama sure knew how to dodge Norman's goofiness without flinching – and that was what counted for me. He got my vote – and even Norman the Republican's vote – that day.

After seeing Edwards, we sat at a table near the cafeteria line. As the media packed up and left, and the rest of the crowd slowly dispersed, Obama stayed for a while. He walked randomly around the room, smiling as he moved from table to table. "I want to talk to the people," he said.

We watched quietly from afar while he circulated freely. He seemed more at ease in this unscripted moment free of journalists than when surrounded by crowds.

We saw Obama again a few years later, by then a Senator. We were at an Urban League dinner as a guest of Norman's office. Norman's company at the time was a donor to the Urban League and had a table reserved at its annual gala, which Norman and Phyllis attended every year.

We were in a crowd waving at Obama, as he was going down an escalator, leaving with his wife, Michelle. We could only see him from a distance, not close enough for Norman to launch one of his famous, or infamous, zingers.

The circus at Manny's now over, Kenny was exhausted from the day's commotion and chaos. He was proud to have distinguished guests but told Norman privately, as we were leaving, he was glad the party was over. It brought fame, Kenny said, not business, to his restaurant. The usual lunch crowd – except for the brave and intrepid like Norman – stayed away that day.

The Tour Guide

"Chicago is the greatest city in the world."
-Norman

The Tour Guide

"I love Chicago. Let me take you around!"
-Norman

Norman loved Chicago. It was more than just his birthplace and hometown. It was his first love. He loved to show off his favorite city to friends and family, and whoever else would listen, even if, sometimes, they were complete strangers. Anybody visiting Chicago for the first time was his victim. They were in for a real treat, his day-long tour.

Chomping on his half-chewed up cigar, he announced to passengers that the car was leaving for their first Chicago adventure: The Norman Tour. They came from around the country, from California and Florida, from Minneapolis and New York, and from overseas: London, Monaco, Germany, and Israel.

The tours started in my childhood in the 1960s and continued until his old age in the 2000s. Every car Norman had owned was blessed at some point to be his tour bus. This was long before MAZLTOV was even in his imagination.

This was Norman's famous Tour of Chicago. Every tour was the same.

It started on the South Side in Hyde Park at the Henry Moore sculpture at the University of Chicago, where the first self-sustained nuclear chain reaction took place. The statue is small and unimposing, an artist's rendering of an atomic mushroom cloud, easy to miss on the open sidewalk, where atomic scientists once worked in secret on the first nuclear bomb, hidden under the bleachers of Stagg Field, a sports field since moved to another location.

But it was part of Chicago, and that was all that mattered to Norman. It didn't matter if a landmark was large or small, significant or not. If it was in Chicago, it was important to Norman. It was just one more thing to brag about his city, the only city that mattered.

While still in Hyde Park, he would pass by the Robie House, an architectural landmark designed by Frank Lloyd Wright, a famous Chicago architect. Wright's masterpieces dot the landscape around Chicago and in suburban Evanston and Oak Park. Norman knew all of them by heart, and he always pointed them out as they popped up along the way.

Chicago is known for its architecture. It was the playground of some of the world's top names in architecture. Besides Wright, there was Mies Van der Rohe and Daniel Burnham. Norman, of course, had to mention this on every tour, name dropping famous architects along the way, as if they were household celebrities. It was just one more gold star for his beloved Chicago.

Norman was a proud card-carrying member of the Chicago Architecture Foundation, today the Chicago Architecture Center. In Norman's day, the foundation offered tours around downtown, showcasing Chicago's architectural landmarks. Today, the Center still offers those tours. Small groups of tourists, each with their own guide, can still be seen around downtown, looking up at the tall buildings from the street or from boats on the Chicago River.

Norman could have easily been one of those guides. Knowing every building downtown personally, historic or not, he would have probably put them to shame.

On his way out of Hyde Park, he would point out the Museum of Science and Industry, now known as the Griffin Museum of Science and Industry, an impressive relic built in Classical Style with Greco-Roman columns for the Columbian Exposition of 1893.

Norman passed the Chicago Fire Department Headquarters on DeKoven, where allegedly Mrs. O'Leary's infamous cow kicked over the lantern starting the Great Chicago Fire of 1871. Norman loved telling visitors that story. It was typical Norman – half-true, half-legend, all tall tale from Norman's repertoire of his city's history.

The Great Chicago Fire was a big part of Norman's tour as he pointed out related landmarks along the way on his northward trek through the city.

Then Norman would swing north up Lake Shore Drive past McCormick Place, Soldier Field, and the Field Museum (where he was also a dues-paying member), the major Chicago landmarks at the southern gateway to downtown.

The tour car continued north along Lake Shore Drive past the Field Museum down a breathtaking promenade up to Randolph Street. Grant Park sat astride the drive, with tall buildings along Michigan Avenue to the west and boats in Monroe Harbor to the east.

Pit stops could be made downtown, by request, at either the John Hancock Center or, what was known then as the Sears Tower (now the Willis Tower), 100-stories each, to get a panoramic view of the city from their observation decks.

While downtown, Norman would explain how "The Loop" got its name from the "L" tracks, the elevated tracks bordering the city center in a perfect square.

Some of Norman's favorite buildings were the Monadnock Building, with its unique stone walls, tapering upward from its wide base. It was a technical feat when designed and built in 1891 by Daniel Burnham, of Columbian Exposition fame. The glass and steel Dirksen Federal Building off Jackson and Dearborn, designed by Mies van der Rohe, were another architectural pride and joy of Norman.

He would try, traffic permitting, to swing by the Board of Trade on LaSalle Street. He pointed up to the statue on top of Ceres, the Roman goddess of agriculture. He told people, incorrectly, it was Athena, the Greek goddess of grain. It was typical Norman. He never let facts get in the way of a good story.

The Art Institute (he was a member there too) on Michigan Avenue was another Norman favorite. He loved telling people that the statues of the two lions in front only roared when a virgin passed by. Norman wasn't sure who made that up, but it sounded good, so he always took credit for it.

It was now time for lunch.

Where would Norman take them? There was only one place he would take them, his holy lunch place, his personal lunchtime culinary shrine, the deli of delis – Manny's. Where else? Going to any other restaurant was unthinkable, even sacrilegious.

After lunch, if the tour attendees weren't exhausted – or ready for a nap from the heavy deli food – it was time to move on. This time up to the North Side.

From there, the Norman bus tour headed north, up Michigan Avenue through The Magnificent Mile. He pointed out the Chicago Water Tower, the only building to survive the Great Chicago Fire, Norman explained, since it was made of stone, not wood, unlike the rest of the city's buildings that burnt to the ground.

Then it was up Lake Shore Drive into Lincoln Park. Along the way, Norman would point at statues in the park of long-gone war heroes and some of Chicago's famous ancestors. He would tell their stories. He knew all of them.

He would work his way past the Lincoln Park Zoo, of which, naturally, he was also a member. The annual black-tie gala at the zoo was one of his obligatory rituals with Phyllis.

Then, it was into the Lincoln Park and Lakeview neighborhoods, where he proudly showed obscure points of interest, known only to Norman, of course, tucked between the gray and brown three-flats.   There was the Alta Vista Terrace, a block-long historic district, where the exterior design of each townhouse is unique but mirrors its counterpart diagonally across the street.

Sometimes, time permitting, or if his guests were interested, he made a stop at the now-closed Oscar Mayer outlet store on Clybourn Avenue for a few frozen hot dogs to go.

Past the city, he would continue north up Sheridan Road into Evanston and Wilmette. Norman impressed visitors with his rendition of how city engineers reversed the flow of the Chicago River in 1900 for flood control and to keep sewage out of Lake Michigan. Norman explained that the small structures visible in the lake from Lake Shore Drive, are called cribs and are part of the city's water management system.

Another part of that system was a canal built between Evanston and Skokie, running from the Chicago River in the city ending up in Wilmette at Gillson Harbor on the lake.

The canal was called the North Shore Channel. Norman called it "Shit Creek," because it was used for treating sewage. He told everybody his famous Shit Creek story. He claimed that once as a kid, he built a raft to cross it. None of his childhood friends can confirm the story – probably just another Norman tall tale.

Across from Gillson Harbor, along Sheridan Road in Wilmette, sits the Baha'i Temple, a beautiful landmark along Chicago's North Shore, and the last stop on Norman's tour.

The tour over, it was time for dinner. Norman took his visitors either to one of his favorite restaurants, or ordered in. He had no choice. Norman couldn't subject his out-of-town guests to a bad meal cooked by Phyllis.

The Roots of Madness I

Why don't you visit me more often?
-Norman's mother, Grandma Ida

"We have family who fought on both sides of the Civil War."
-Norman flinging a tall tale of bullshit

Norman's mother, Ida – always Grandma Ida to me – was a house on fire. It was a fire Norman caught early on. Grandma Ida passed on to Norman her outgoing nature and love of being social. They were both the life of the party and commanded immediate attention when they walked in a room. They both had boundless energy.

They both liked being out there, and out there they were, literally and figuratively, in more ways than one. Eccentric and offbeat, energetic and unstoppable, Grandma Ida and her son, Norman, together or separately, were known wherever they went. They were always both in the limelight.

They were also both fiercely independent. Nobody was going to tell Grandma Ida, and later Norman, where to go or what to do – or who to socialize with. They didn't follow anybody's rules. They made the rules.

Grandma Ida seemed to be the boss, wherever she went. Though not particularly religious, she regularly attended the synagogues where she lived in Joliet, Illinois, and St. Paul, Minnesota. Just as her son went to restaurants not for food, but to meet people, Grandma Ida likewise went to synagogues not to pray, but to build her social network.

The rabbi? What rabbi? Ask Grandma Ida. She was the real sheriff in town at the synagogue, and she wanted everybody to know it. She was fearless when giving a piece of her mind to any rabbi in her path. No rabbi was going to push Grandma Ida around. Later, Norman too, struck fear in rabbis who dared to cross him. It was just something else he picked up from her.

I always suspected she secretly ran the synagogue or, at least, maybe just the Sisterhood, the official name for the women's organization at many synagogues in Grandma Ida's day.

Like Norman in Chicago, she seemed to know everyone in Joliet and St. Paul. The synagogue for Grandma Ida, like restaurants for Norman, was just one of her many local powerbases.

Grandma Ida lived a hundred years. And what a century it was. She lived through the Titanic, two world wars, both the Korean and Vietnam wars and, in between, the 1918 flu epidemic, Prohibition, and the Great Depression. She was young enough to see silent movies and old enough to see computers. She grew up before dial phones and grew old with cell phones.

Grandma Ida proudly told everybody she was one of the first women to vote in 1928, a right granted to women in America only a few years earlier, though she couldn't recall – or didn't want to say – who she voted for.

On the personal side, she outlived three husbands and helped run her immigrant father's cap factory in the 1920s, and later her own gift shop.

Then, of course, in the middle of it all, while working at the cap factory, she had her only child, Norman. A sister, who would have been my aunt and who I'll never know, died in infancy a year before Norman was born.

Grandma Ida may have aged physically, but not emotionally. She was the same spry and combative lady well into old age. Her toughness didn't diminish with age.

She drove on her own to her ninetieth birthday party and danced and sang with relatives who were decades younger, some of whom flew to St. Paul for the occasion. Still driving a few years later at ninety-four, she got a speeding ticket. She lived on her own, cooking and baking for herself until the age of ninety-five, when, amazingly, she finally succumbed to old age, terrorizing the nursing home where she ended up.

Whenever I visited, she baked a box of her famous lemon squares and thimble cookies – usually a huge box I couldn't schlep on the plane. She made the thimble cookies by pressing her thumb into circular pieces of cookie dough and dropping in a dab of jelly. She loved sweets and, if she didn't like something in a gift box, she would put the half-eaten piece of candy back in the box, hoping no one would see. But we always saw, and we always let it go.

She kept her family on their toes and entertained – often driving them nuts – along the way. She was a battle ax who nagged Norman nonstop. "Hey, Norman, let's do . . ." "Hey, Norman, take me to . . ." "Hey, Norman, what do you think of going to . . ." "Hey, Norman, stop doing that." "Hey, Norman, come to Joliet on Sunday for dinner." Then, later, "Hey, Norman, come see your mother in St. Paul."

"Norman this . . ." "Norman that . . ." "Norman . . ." "Norman . . ." "Norman . . ." Oh my God, it was endless.

"Mom, you're driving me crazy," he used to say angrily on the phone, while chomping on his cigar stub to calm down.

I often wondered whether she lived so long because of her energy, her stubbornness or because she was just a pain-in-the-ass, a lovable pain-in-the-ass at that, but still a pain-in-the-ass.

Grandma Ida trained Norman well for life with Phyllis, to whom she passed the Torch of Nagging. It was like an Olympic torch, since it took an athlete to survive the constant hounding and nudging. Norman won the Gold Medal in the Nagging Survival Marathon.

The roots of Norman's madness went beyond Grandma Ida. They go back to his immigrant roots in the *shtetl*, a Yiddish word for the Jewish ghettos in Europe, and to Galicia. In Russia, that *shtetl* was known as the Pale of Settlement.

The story starts in 1881, when Czar Alexander II was assassinated in Russia. The Jews, of course, were blamed, as they always were for every calamity in Russia back them. The Jewish ties to the conspirators were weak, if any, at all. But it didn't matter. In the eyes of the assassinated czar's son and successor, Alexander III, Jews were the problem, the root of all evil. They had to be dealt with.

Norman's ancestors didn't hang around to see the new czar's plans for the Jews. The mere thought of an orgy of antisemitic violence tearing through Russia was enough to scare them. It was ethnic cleansing before the term became fashionable.

Norman descended from two Russian Jewish families, Bisno and his namesake, Dubin. Once they left and came here, they cut all ties with their former homeland. That was the extent of Norman's ties to Russia. In the *shtetl*, where they lived, they weren't part of Russian society, anyways. With their own culture and language and, of course, religion – strict Orthodox Judaism – they were total outsiders. Russia was an unwelcoming and belligerent host, especially to its Jewish residents.

Whenever Norman saw Russia or the Soviet Union in the news on TV, decrepit and with all its problems, he would always say, "I'm glad my great-grandparents had the brains to get on that boat."

Against this backdrop, it was Sholom Bisno, Norman's great-grandfather, who stepped on that boat in Hamburg and headed for the US. He was one of four Bisno brothers who made their way to the States. He took the family, including Norman's grandmother, Celia, an infant, to Atlanta. The family stayed there about a year, before moving to Chicago in 1883.

Norman's great-grandfather on the Dubin side left Russia around the same time as the Bisno family. They weren't as lucky as Sholom. Norman's great-great-grandfather, who supposedly was a tax collector for some unknown nobleman, was brutally murdered by Cossack soldiers in a pogrom. That was the family's signal it was time to get out of town and head for America. They eventually settled in Gary, Indiana, and started a small business. Their son, Sam Dubin, was the Corporation Counsel for Gary for several decades.

On the Bisno side, Sholom's daughter, Celia, married Isadore "Ike" Brandy in Chicago in 1903. A picture from the wedding, from somewhere in the immigrant neighborhood on Roosevelt Road, sat on Norman's shelf. They stood there solemnly, not smiling, in the formal attire of the day, Ike in a vest and white gloves and Celia holding a bouquet, the custom in the spooky black-and-white photos of the early Twentieth Century.

That ancient photo was my earliest childhood memory of my long-gone ancestors. Celia lived long enough for me to meet her. My relationship with Grandma Brandy, as I called her, was brief, since she died when I was five years old and was too sick to talk or have any kind of relationship.

Norman inherited many of Ike's traits, passing them down to me, as well. He was friendly and knew a lot of people. He was a wheeler-dealer and a master networker. He knew how to build relationships. Yet, he was still fiercely independent, like Norman and myself. He believed in hard work and building businesses and had an entrepreneurial bent.

Norman didn't know much about Ike's past or where he came from. He knew Ike somehow got to Chicago by himself as a child or young teenager from Galicia, a province of the pre-World War I Austro-Hungarian Empire in Central Europe. Otherwise, Ike was completely on his own with no other family here.

Ike was a *Galitzianer*, the Yiddish name for people from Galicia. *Galitzianers* were one of Eastern Europe's biggest Jewish tribes and were concentrated in Austro-Hungary to the south, while the *Litvaks*, the other big Jewish tribe, were from Poland and further north.

Galitzianers were known for their warmth and sense of humor, a trait handed down to Norman.

After introducing himself first as a bank robber, Norman then proudly told everybody he was a *Galitzianer*. Most people, unless they were from a similar Ashkenazi Jewish background, had no idea what he was talking about. As usual, people politely played along with the friendly stranger.

Ike peddled fruit on Roosevelt Road from a cart in the 1890s. One day his heel somehow got wedged under the cart, and it rolled over him, crushing one leg. He survived but lost the leg. He had a wooden leg strapped to his body for the rest of his life.

Phyllis told me she once saw the thick leather strap of Ike's wooden leg slung over his shoulder, when he took off his shirt. The wooden leg was Ike's symbol. It was a symbol of his strength. It was also Norman's image of Ike. He talked about it whenever Ike's name came up.

Ike was tough. The wooden leg didn't stop him from getting married, raising two daughters and building an extremely successful cap factory.

Unlike Celia, I never met Ike. He died a month before I was born. Norman made sure I still knew all about Ike, even if, for me, he was just the stuff of family lore and legend. To this day, I feel his presence, as if I had known him personally.

Ike spoke with a thick Yiddish accent, I was told. When he talked about the part of the Bisno clan who settled in Kenosha, he used to say they lived in Kenosha *"Gonsin,"* how he said "Wisconsin" in his heavily accented English.

Ike was a loyal reader of the Forward, the leading Yiddish daily newspaper in the US, but was illiterate in English his whole life. Grandma Ida had to read every document and contract in English to Ike. Like all immigrants, Ike wanted to be American and only wanted to speak English, not Yiddish, at home. Grandma Ida never picked up this rich and colorful language. She didn't need to. She expressed herself quite well in her own colorful English.

Grandma Ida was born in 1905, the oldest of Ike and Celia's two daughters. She inherited his pluck and energy. Somehow, it's not entirely clear, Ike built a cap business in the factory district on the near West Side somewhere off Roosevelt Road, just west of downtown Chicago. How he went from street peddler to factory owner is lost to history.

But the business was enormously successful, as caps were the attire *de jour* in the early Twentieth Century, and Ike prospered. Ike was extremely generous and made sure Grandma Ida and her sister, Rose, lived well.

Ike apparently had a side business lending money, which Norman never talked about. I only heard about it once when someone came up to Norman at Manny's and told a story how his grandfather owed Norman's grandfather Ike money in the old days back on Roosevelt Road. He said his grandfather had to pay up or suffer some unknown fate under the terms of Ike's "Five on Friday" loan. Norman refused to tell me what Five on Friday was, and I didn't push the matter. It was the only deep dark family secret Norman ever hid from me.

Grandma Ida worked in the front office of Ike's factory as a young woman in the 1920s when a guy named Dubin walked in looking for a job. He apparently charmed her enough that they got married. It was a short marriage, during which Norman was born. Though they divorced when Norman was a baby, he still kept in touch with his father and a few other members of the Dubin family throughout his life. But it was the Bisno side he was closest to.

As a single mother, Grandma Ida had to work and was away a lot. Norman was raised by his Ike and Celia. They all lived together in Uptown on the North Side of Chicago. Ike's successful business helped them weather the Depression.

Norman picked up social skills in the neighborhood. Grandma Ida's sister, my Aunt Rose, had two sons, Stuart and Stanley, and lived across the street. Stanley was the same age as Norman, while Stuart was seven years younger. He and Stanley used to play practical jokes on Stuart when he was an infant. They apparently once scooped some yellow baby food from a jar and spread it on the carpet and told Aunt Rose that Stuart had pooped on the floor.

Then there were his neighbors David and Angelo. The three playmates were The Three Musketeers on the block. They were inseparable. Angelo was the son of immigrants from Greece, and David lived next door to Norman with his Aunt Min. David had been sent by his parents in London to live with Min during the bombing of Britain in World War II. David and his aunt were also Jewish, though, like Norman and Ida, not observant.

Norman showed promise as an accountant at an early age. He managed the accounts receivable for a comic book business Angelo started. Later, Angelo recalled they were in a school play together, Snow White and the Seven Dwarfs. Angelo played Sneezy, and Norman was Sleepy. Apparently, they had a lot of laughs along the way.

Celia still kept a tight leash on Norman as a child, not letting him out much and restricting who he could play with when he was out. Norman finally broke free when he grew up and left home. His innate social nature bubbled to the surface with a vengeance. He went out to make love to the world and meet as many people as he could. Norman wanted to be everybody's friend.

In the meantime, union organizers tried to set up shop in Ike's plant. Ike was fiercely anti-union and wouldn't budge. Ike personally knew Abraham Bisno, Celia's cousin and a famous union organizer in Chicago in the early Twentieth Century. Obviously, the two didn't get along and, I was told, they wouldn't speak to each other at family dinners.

The union organizers persisted and threatened to burn down Ike's factory. He sold the business just before the war to a clothing company, which made a fortune manufacturing uniforms for soldiers. I often speculated if he stayed in business, Norman would have inherited and taken over the business, eventually passing it down to me. I would have been the third generation in a family clothing business.

During the war, after Ike left the cap business, he was still a *hondler*, Yiddish for a wheeler-dealer. Nobody had connections like Ike. When his girls, Ida and Rose, wanted rationed items, like nylons, Ike somehow found them. Ike could get anything. Rations were no barrier to Ike.

The cap factory gone, the ration business over, fate had other plans for Norman.

After the war ended, Norman graduated from Senn High School. Angelo moved out, went to the University of Chicago, and got married. He worked his way up the corporate ladder to become an executive. David went back to the UK, and Norman lost touch with him for twenty years – until Grandma Ida showed up on his doorstep in London.

By that time, David had built an enormously successful manufacturing business.

Ike and Celia moved briefly to Arizona and Norman followed them for a while. They came back to Chicago after almost getting killed in a car accident. Norman remembered them doing rehab themselves at home with pulleys attached to bags of bricks. The Bisno toughness saved them.

When Norman returned to Chicago, he went to De Paul University and lived at the ZBT fraternity house at the University of Chicago. At ZBT, a Jewish fraternity, Norman met Bob, Frank, and Norm, friends he kept for life. They all got married around the same time after graduating in the early 1950s and, shortly afterward, starting raising families.

Norman and Phyllis married in 1951 and went to Osceola, for their honeymoon to see their Southern cousins, Lionel and Nora. Apparently, they almost dodged a snow storm along the way after Norman had trouble starting the car. They told me it was quite an adventure.

There must have been something about Norman and Phyllis driving in snow storms. Years later, when coming back from visiting the Kanter family in St. Paul, they got stuck in a snow storm while driving to the airport. The road was blocked by a drift, and they had to go back to the hotel for another few nights.

I was born on a frigid bitter Chicago day in January. Phyllis's mother, Ethel, called me "Little Two Below," the first of many nicknames I would have throughout my life. Norman and Phyllis had been married five years, and thought, at first, they wouldn't be able to have kids. Then, surprise. I arrived.

When I was a kid, Norman and Phyllis went out a lot with his former ZBT frat brothers and their wives. Their kids were like my cousins. We went to each other's houses and ordered in, or went to restaurants as a group. We all remained lifelong friends, Norman with his frat buddies and I with their kids.

Grandma Ida picked up her life again, marrying Irving in Joliet. They ran a gift shop together, which closed after several years in business. Grandma Ida used to give me trinkets from the shop she had stored in her basement, whenever I visited Joliet with Norman and Phyllis.

They didn't have kids of their own, but Grandma Ida was close to Irving's daughter Judy and her husband Harry, a physics professor in New York.

Harry was every bit a European gentleman, looking the part of a professor with a goatee and a receding hair line. He left Vienna barely escaping the Holocaust and learned to speak perfect English without even a hint of an accent, adding to his native German and flawless French. I have remained friends with their son, Larry, who also lives in New York.

Harry was very fascinating. It was always a treat when he came to town. We would talk about his work as a physicist, or about Europe and the gourmet European restaurant he dreamed of opening on a boat in the Hudson River near his house. He bought me my first set of encyclopedias, when Brittanica was the standard in every educated person's home.

In 1965, exactly twenty years after the end of the Second World War, Grandma Ida and Irving went to France and England on vacation. Norman hadn't heard from David since he went back to London after the war. Grandma Ida looked him up and found him.

By that time, David had built a successful business and, it turned out, was doing business in the States and visited Chicago regularly. David and Norman were reunited and saw each other regularly whenever David came to town, or when Norman went to London.

Irving passed away after they were married over thirty years. But, Grandma Ida, as expected, didn't sit still. She met Sam during a trip to Florida, and he soon after became her third husband. Sam was from St. Paul. Grandma Ida packed her bags and left Joliet for St. Paul.

Grandma Ida was seventy-three when she got married again. Norman flew up to St. Paul for the ceremony. There he was, giving away the bride – his mother – something he never expected.

Sam had four grown kids, Yale, Myrna, Doreen, and Bernie, all married and all with their own kids, making for a large and warm Jewish family. Their spouses, respectively, were Jeanne, Tony, Barney, and Sheila.

The Kanter family was a big warm Jewish family with lots of kids, cousins, and in-laws, enough to keep Grandma Ida busy every day and social every weekend, just as she liked it. Her turf as family *yenta*, Yiddish for a busybody, expanded greatly beyond just the two-person Norman and Phyllis Show.

They adopted Grandma Ida as their own *bubbe*, Yiddish for grandmother. They also took Norman and Phyllis in as their unofficial fifth sibling and spouse.

Sam was a soft spoken and sweet guy, who immigrated to Canada from Eastern Europe as a teenager, and still spoke with a thick Yiddish accent. Grandma Ida was the boss of the house, but Sam seemed to enjoy every moment reporting for duty.

Between all the bar and bat mitzvahs and weddings, we made plenty of family trips with Norman and Phyllis to St. Paul and to Canada, where two of Sam's children still lived.

Nothing stopped Grandma Ida. Nothing. Not even a pacemaker. On a trip with Sam to Toronto to see Myrna's family, she passed out in Eaton Centre, a large shopping mall downtown. She was taken to the hospital and given a pacemaker. She had driven herself and Sam from St. Paul to Toronto, through Chicago and around Lake Michigan to Detroit and into Canada.

Grandma Ida was nearly eighty at the time. Norman asked me to fly to Toronto and drive Sam back in their car to St. Paul. Ida would fly back later, when she was better.

At the border, we waited forever in a busy line. So far, so good. All routine. Then a US immigration officer approached our car. This was pre-9/11, when they just asked you where you were from, and if you named an American city and had no foreign accent, they waved you through. I said Chicago, then the officer asked Sam, "Where are you from?" I quickly answered "He's from Chicago too," trying to cut him off. Sam, whose hearing was fading, said in a pea-thick Yiddish accent, *"Vats he sayin over der?"*

That was it. The immigration officer, told us to pull over, and asked us for IDs. They inspected the car, opening the trunk and the hood and all four doors. Satisfied I wasn't illegally smuggling old Jewish men into the country, they let us go, and we crossed over to Detroit without incident.

Grandma Ida fully recovered from her pacemaker surgery and lived a full life. Sadly, Sam passed away only a few years after they married. Grandma Ida stayed in St. Paul, now a fully ensconced member of the Kanter family.

Even without Sam, Grandma Ida – and her pacemaker – was as crazy as ever in St. Paul. She was busy not only with the synagogue but volunteered to help Hmong refugees and Jewish immigrants from Russia. She attended every Kanter family event and dinner, of which there were many.

Grandma Ida drove like a bat out of hell. At ninety-four, a cop pulled her over for speeding. "You can't give an old lady a ticket," she said. "Oh, yes, I can," he said, and gave it to her anyways.

Shortly afterward, she decided, on her own, without prodding from anyone in the family, to give up the keys. She called me and offered to give me her car. I thanked her profusely for her generosity but politely told her I didn't need another car.

A week later, a check suddenly appeared in the mail from her for five hundred dollars. She had apparently sold the car and sent me the money without telling me. A nice loving touch I never forgot.

Nature took its course and at ninety-five, Grandma Ida started to fail. She was forgetting to take her medication and was confused all the time. It was time for Norman to come up to St. Paul and take her back to Chicago to put her in a nursing home. He got her dressed and escorted her on the short plane flight.

Before she arrived, Norman had already reserved a spot for Grandma Ida at a nearby nursing home.

The nursing home should have boarded up its windows in preparation for the oncoming storm, Hurricane Grandma Ida, was about to hit.

When Grandma Ida arrived, she was still somewhat lucid. After Norman dropped her off, she went from room to room, saying, "Anybody that can walk and see, we're getting out of here." She, and the posse of a dozen people she rounded up, was only stopped by a surprised security guard at the front door.

Another time, Grandma Ida stood in front of the cafeteria at dinner and thanked everybody for coming to the wedding. Whenever Norman visited, she would lean over and whisper in his ear, "I need some cash to tip the waiters here." She once told Norman she was getting on the train the next day to go to Osceola to see the cousins there.

Grandma Ida asked me once why my brother (I'm an only child) never visited, and how the restaurant business (I've never owned a restaurant) was doing. I said my brother was busy, and the restaurant was doing fine. Arguing with someone with dementia was pointless.

When Grandma Ida was ninety-eight, she told me she needed a man. I told her I had the perfect guy. He was 102 years old and Jewish. I said he was a little slow, but we could pump him up with Viagra, and that he would be good to go. She didn't answer. She was already too far gone.

When Grandma Ida died at a hundred, Norman gave a stirring eulogy at the gravesite, saying everything in her life was "*bashert*," Yiddish for destiny. God must have been whispering in his ear, since Norman wasn't normally so articulate or serious.

With Grandma Ida's passing, the only aggravation remaining for Norman was his wife, Phyllis.

The Roots of Madness II

"If a married man has an opinion and walks into a forest alone, is he still wrong?"
-Norman

The Roots of Madness II

"Shut up, Norman!"
-Phyllis

If Norman's mother wasn't enough to drive him batty, it was his wife, Phyllis, who pushed him over the edge.

Phyllis was a stereotypical Jewish mother, right out of central casting. She was a little crazy, a little neurotic, a little hysterical, but above all the only mother who could love someone kooky and quirky like me. She was always there for me with words of encouragement and support.

Phyllis still was as goofy as Norman. They were a perfect match. Sara and I didn't have to go to the theater. They entertained us with their own drama. The Norman and Phyllis Show was nonstop entertainment, day or night.

Sometimes Sara would wake up laughing in the middle of the night for no reason. It was always something Norman and Phyllis had said, or done, at dinner a few hours earlier.

Phyllis was short in stature but tall in strength. Two months before my bar mitzvah, she was almost killed in an auto accident. A speeding car rammed into her car as she pulled into a busy intersection in Skokie. The offender had sped up as the yellow light was changing to red. He broadsided her in what could have been a fatal blow.

Phyllis's car spun out of control in the middle of traffic and, miraculously, didn't hit anything, or anybody. The car carrying a severely wounded Phyllis landed on an empty corner. She survived only to be bedridden for over a month with three broken ribs.

Amazingly, she recovered – unaided with no walker or wheelchair – in time to attend my bar mitzvah. She lived another fifty years most of it with chronic back pain from the accident.

Shut Up, Norman!

Phyllis's physical strength was only matched by her screaming ability. Never cross Phyllis. She always put Norman in his place with a resounding "Shut up, Norman" that sent me running for cover.   Her strong lungs made up for her small size.

In fact, she started many conversations with Norman with just "Shut up, Norman." It was how she greeted him. It was her mating call, in a perverse way, a shriek before the attack. Once the territory was secure, she would keep yelling to drive the point home. Norman just ignored her. He sat quietly in his favorite chair in another room, reading The Wall Street Journal.

Phyllis was perpetually at a baseline level of hysteria. She used to ask some of the craziest questions. I learned early on how to respond.

Well, Is She Jewish? Are You Having Sex Yet?

When I met Sara, Phyllis was dying to know if she was Jewish. Instead of just asking me directly, it came out hysterically as "Well, does she have parents?" I answered, "No. She came in by parachute."

Phyllis had other real gems for Sara. The questions about Sara never stopped. She really wanted to know if I was sleeping with her. This is an absolutely vital piece of information for every Jewish mother. They have to know when their kids are having sex. It would be too tacky to just come out and ask, "Well, are you having sex?" Jewish mothers are clever. They ask in a roundabout way.

Phyllis asked me, instead, "Do you drive her home?" I replied, "No. I drive and she runs alongside the car."

Phyllis wasn't satisfied. The matter still hadn't been settled.

Phyllis got her answer when Sara and I traveled with Norman and Phyllis to a wedding. Sara and I stayed in the same hotel room – not with Norman and Phyllis, of course – and Phyllis pointed at two single beds in the hotel room and said, "I'll bet you two slept together in that bed and messed up the other one just to fool me." How did she know?

Phyllis never brought the subject up again. She didn't have to. There were just too many other more pressing, and embarrassing, questions for Sara.

When Phyllis saw my bikini-style underwear, she asked Sara, "How does he pee in those things? It doesn't have a slit in front." Sara just laughed and said, "This one is for you, Joel."

The crazy questions never ceased.

Phyllis asked me when I called her during a trip to France – a country known for its food – "Are you eating?" I said, "Of course not. I gave that up years ago." Before another business trip to London, she asked, "Are you bringing a clean shirt?" I answered, "No, of course, not. I went through my dirty laundry and picked out only my most wrinkled and dirty shirts."

Phyllis had the same beehive hairdo since 1964, when the fad started. As she got older, it shrunk a bit, but it was still there long into old age. I never really understood what they did every week at the hairdresser, a sacrosanct ritual every Saturday.

It looked like all they did was pump more fiberglass into her hair to keep the structure up. Every time I touched it, it bounced back. She yelled, "Don't touch my hair." Once after a hairdresser visit, Norman said he saw worms growing in her hair. She yelled.

Phyllis's Weekly Culinary Nightmare

Phyllis was a lousy cook. She hated to cook. It was something else to scream about.

Most people say, "Just like my mother used to cook," I used to say, "Just like my mother didn't use to cook."

Phyllis's specialty was instant and powdered crap, anything in a can or a box, where just water could be added, and it could be thrown in the oven or tossed on the stove. Most of the time, I just wanted to toss it right into the garbage.

Baking? Cookies could be bought. Why try to make something when you can buy it already prepared? She wouldn't have been able to bake anyways. Pouring things into measuring cups, which could have spilled on the counter, would have messed up her anal-retentive kitchen.

Microwave ovens didn't exist when I was growing up. If they did, Phyllis probably would have mastered them. When I was out of the house, and Norman bought his first microwave, she yelled at him whenever he tried to use it. She had to be the master of her own kitchen, as unstocked as it was with good food.

Phyllis had the same rigid menu for decades.

I still remember it clearly. They say you forget trauma. Not Phyllis's cooking. It has stuck with me since childhood – it still comes up on me, when I think about it – like belching and indigestion.

Monday night was alternating hamburger or meatloaf (basically the same thing in different life forms). Tuesday night was chicken. Wednesday night was corn giblets. Thursday night was tuna salad and, finally, to top off the weekly culinary feast, Friday was steak. Portions were small and the food was bad.

A brave guest who once survived Phyllis's cooking thought she rationed food. He called the small amount of food on his plate "Phyllis Portions."

Norman got so used to the menu, he would walk in the door and say, "Phyllis, what's for dinner? Wait, let me guess. It's Wednesday. It must be corn giblets." Phyllis always answered with her customary "Shut up, Norman."

Norman had a little ritual every night before dinner. He would have a shot of Kettle One and some peanuts. It was his way of coping with the meal about to be served.

When I grew up and left the house, I was shocked to learn not everybody ate packaged or powdered food. "I don't believe it," Phyllis said, when I came to visit. "He eats." Phyllis was mystified by my eating habits as a child. She thought I had an eating disorder. It never dawned on her that it was her cooking.

Norman and I got a reprieve on the weekends, when we either ate out or ordered in. She only shined in the kitchen in those off times when she could order in. She was a magician with a telephone, not the skillet.

Phyllis ruled over the kitchen, as if it was her kingdom, without mastering it. She had a spot reserved for everything in the refrigerator. If someone dared put something in outside of its assigned space, she would scream it didn't belong and would move it over to her preferred location, even if only one inch over.

Phyllis once complained that Norman never helped her in the kitchen, and then when he did, she yelled at him for getting the sink wet. Norman once told her he had a surprise for her in a kitchen cabinet. She asked what it was. He said he left her a crumb. She yelled.

Phyllis also had a mystical attachment to her car, even though she never drove it. When it was stolen, she cried, "Somebody has my baby." A few days, later, the police saw the car during a traffic stop and the driver tried to speed away. The car was totaled after crashing during a high-speed chase. Phyllis wanted to sit Shiva, the Jewish funeral visitation, for the car.

Norman went to court when the suspect was arrested. He stood up and spoke, trying to cut off the prosecutor. Norman, the good citizen, just had to say a few words. The judge told him to sit down and be quiet and let the prosecutor present the case.

Phyllis's Bowel Movements and Kvetching Family

Bodily functions, especially bowel movements, were Phyllis's favorite topic of conversation. The refrigerator was fully stocked with bottles of prune juice, enough for a nuclear war. She drank it faithfully every morning to ward off the "Greenberg Stomach," some mysterious intestinal ailment, inherited from her ancestors on her mother's side, particularly her hypochondriac Aunt Pearl.

Everybody in the family knew to never ask Aunt Pearl how she was. She would give a half-hour litany of her latest medical tests from her blood pressure to her Pap smear.

Aunt Pearl's sister was Ethel, Phyllis's mother. When Ethel came to town, she had her own strange habits. One day, I heard someone snorting in the kitchen. I saw someone hunched over the open refrigerator door. I didn't recognize who it was until I got closer. Ethel was sniffing bottles of spicy horse radish.

"It clears my sinuses," Ethel said. At least, Phyllis had stocked up enough prune juice for them both before Ethel's arrival.

Phyllis came from a long line of whiners, complainers and *kvetches*, Yiddish for a whiner. If there was an illness, she had it, and it was probably fatal.

Norman and Phyllis ended up taking care of Aunt Pearl when she was elderly. Norman got so tired of her whining, he once told her, "One more peep out of you, and I'm going to make an appointment with Dr. Kevorkian." Kevorkian was the infamous assisted-suicide doctor at the time.

Phyllis's Unknown Ancestors

Unlike Norman's family, little is known about Phyllis's ancestors. Like Norman's family, they came from Russia, but about twenty years later, sometime in the early Twentieth Century. They survived pogroms in Russia only to perish, nearly wiped out, in fact, in the 1918 flu epidemic, leaving Grandma Ethel as the head of the household at an early age.

Supposedly, they had an unpronounceable last name and were dubbed "Greenberg" by an anonymous official on Ellis Island. Greenberg might have come from the nickname "greenie" given to new Jewish arrivals, because they were considered "green" right off the boat.

I often wondered if Phyllis's surviving family became germophobes, and then hypochondriacs, because of the flu epidemic. I'll never really know.

Soup Gives Me Gas and How to Flush the Toilet

When a waiter asked Phyllis, if she wanted soup or salad, she put her fingers on her abdomen and said, "Soup gives me gas." The waiter didn't react. He didn't say anything. He must have heard this before.

Shortly after Phyllis broke her right wrist in a fall, we were at a big family gathering at a restaurant in Chicago. There were relatives and cousins from around the country sitting around a huge round table. Everybody was talking. It was very noisy. Phyllis sat quietly for a while. Then she proudly held up her bandage in the air for everybody to see. She blurted out over the conversation, "You know I have to flush the toilet now with my left hand." The table went dead silent. Nobody knew what to say. How do you follow that?

Phyllis was the quintessential Skokie housewife. She wore the standard uniform at home, a housecoat and slippers. This is my childhood image of her. This is how she was dressed when she ran around the house after me. When Sara and I saw the play Diary of a Skokie Housewife in the 1990s – at a theater in Skokie, of course – I was horrified. They had Phyllis pegged to a T. How did they know Phyllis so well?

Also, typical of the housewife era, Phyllis watched the daily soaps in the afternoon, while cleaning the house. Her favorites were As the World Turns, which I called As the Stomach Turns, since it nauseated me, and The Old and the Lethargic, my nickname for The Young and the Restless. She would call her mother Ethel, also an avid soap watcher, and talk about who was sleeping with whom on the shows.

The Mad Scientist Blows a Fuse

Phyllis also put up with my mad scientist projects. I once built a simulated tornado with a vacuum cleaner, a fan and a pan of water. Of course, in order to be efficient, I had to plug everything into one socket. I turned on my contraption in the basement, and a little funnel cloud of water rose from the pan.

I got the plans for the tornado from Scientific American, my favorite childhood magazine. I just had to do it. I really had wanted to build the home-sized nuclear reactor they featured one month, but we didn't have all parts in the house. Just as well, since I don't think the neighbors would have appreciated being irradiated. So, I had to settle for the artificial tornado in the basement.

Then, boom, all the lights in the house went out. I had blown a fuse. The whole house went dark. I could hear the pitter patter, or rather the pounding, of Phyllis's slippers on the floor above me. She yelled from the top of the stairs, "What the hell are you doing down there?"

Fortunately, Norman, no Mr. Handyman, I might add, figured out how to turn on the switch in the fuse box, and all was good with the universe. Not before Phyllis first let out a barrage of screaming and yelling.

Phyllis the Small Town Cookie

Phyllis was born in Joliet in 1929 just before the Great Depression. Joliet was a thriving industrial town at the time and not really rural, but to Phyllis it was a small town, especially compared to Chicago, where she eventually lived all her life with Norman.

"I'm just a small town cookie," she used to tell everybody.

Her brother, my uncle Ronnie, eventually joined the Navy, became a lawyer and moved to Long Beach, California, where he was a prosecutor. At the same time, he remained a reservist in the Naval Judge Advocate Group, also known as the JAG corp.

Ronnie was a loyal Navy guy and eventually retired at the rank of Captain, one step below an Admiral. Norman, of course, told everybody, "My brother-in-law the admiral." Just another of Norman's tall tales.

Phyllis and Norman were high school sweethearts and married after Norman finished college at DePaul. Phyllis went to the University of Illinois but didn't graduate. After they married, she never worked again. They were the stereotypical suburban couple with the house, the car and the kid, me.

Phyllis was always there for me. She always came through in tough times. Whether it was a kind word of encouragement when I was down, praise when I succeeded in some venture or got an award or wrote my first book, a hug when I needed emotional support, money when my car suddenly broke down, or just a warm glance in my direction.

"I'm just doing the best I can," Phyllis used to always say, shaking her head.

Norman wasn't surprised when I started traveling the world and even lived overseas for a while. He blamed my wanderlust on the enclosed playpen where Phyllis put me all day as an infant. Norman, the amateur Freud, concluded my desire to travel stemmed from trying to escape that playpen, which he compared to a makeshift jail cell in the middle of the living room.

Besides being an amateur psychotherapist, Norman practiced medicine without a license, dispensing medical advice to friends and family. If anybody asked, I said he went to the best medical school advertised on the cover of a matchbook.

On the Road with Norman and Phyllis

Traveling by car with Norman and Phyllis, well, to put it bluntly, was a trip. Between Norman getting lost and stopping for directions and not listening, and Phyllis yelling at him, road trips were enjoyable and relaxing.

At some point, I became the designated back seat navigator, paper maps in hand, in the prehistoric times before Google and cellphones, to keep Norman on track and Phyllis quiet. I collected maps as a kid, like a true aficionado, along with rocks, stamps, and coins.

On a trip to a wedding in Baltimore, the same wedding where Phyllis figured out Sara and I were sleeping in the same bed, Norman rented a car. Norman thought we needed gas. He pulled into a gas station and, lo and behold, the tank was already full. He had read the gas gauge incorrectly.

As we're pulling out, Sara noticed the hood was loose. Norman said it was fine. He didn't notice. It suddenly popped all the way open, blocking the windshield, and we had to pull over. He had accidentally pulled the lever to open the hood, thinking it was the gas tank. He got out and shut the hood.

Ready to rock and roll, and roll we did, right past the hotel. Norman saw the hotel driveway pass by and, amazingly without backing into anyone or getting into an accident, screeched on the brakes and went backward into the curved driveaway.

Surprisingly, other than Phyllis's occasional complaints about this that or the other – or her shock about Sara and I in bed together – the rest of the trip went without incident.

The Origin of the Restaurant Circuit

Phyllis and Norman went to restaurants every Saturday and Sunday night as long as I can remember. They had no choice. Seven days in a row of Phyllis's cooking would have killed Norman before his time.

I started going to restaurants with them when I was around ten years old. When Sara and I got married, we went out with them a lot.

I knew they felt comfortable around Sara, when Phyllis and Norman started acting naturally in front of her – Phyllis yelling "Shut up, Norman" and Norman ignoring her.

Phyllis is Always Right

Norman taught me the dynamics of marriage early on – the wife is always right. He never argued with Phyllis. He couldn't. She was always right. She always knew the answer to everything.

Norman and Phyllis had a fiftieth anniversary bash in 2001 at Chez Joel (not related to me) on Taylor Street.

"Phyllis is always right," Norman said in his speech. "How could I always be wrong for fifty years?"

Norman's wisdom, and my own experience married for thirty years plus to Sara, inspired me to write my book, Yes Dear! A Husband's Guide to Marriage.

Phyllis the Sex Goddess

During a vacation with David in Monaco, where every woman, including those that shouldn't, went topless on the beach, Phyllis took off her top. Norman showed me a photo of Phyllis smiling and topless, laying on the beach. I tried to focus on her beehive hairdo. I was too shocked to look at anything else. I've been traumatized ever since.

Sitting in the back seat of the car, as a kid, Norman once turned to Phyllis and said, "You know, Phyllis, you talk too much and f--- to little." "Shut up,

Norman," she said. It was just another fond memory from my childhood of The Norman and Phyllis Show.

Some people told me they couldn't imagine Phyllis having sex. It would mess up her hair.

They were wrong.

It was the other side of Phyllis I didn't know about, or didn't want to know about, either.

Looking back, Norman's obscene comment was a little odd. When he died, many years later, I found a stash of blue Viagra pills scattered in the top drawer of his dresser. I finally understood what Phyllis meant, in Norman's later years, when she said, "Norman is now ready again for the big time."

I also found, after he died, a file full of porn pictures on his laptop. They were all pictures of Black women. He had told me once in passing he had a thing for Black women. It was just another of the many kooky things I sometimes ignored. Then I thought for a second. Black women? Maybe Sheldon, the Black waiter at Gibsons, really was my half-brother.

The Anti-Suburbanite

"I'm not talking to Stormy's father again."
-Norman about a neighbor he disliked

"I think we can save the lawn."
-Norman's landscaper about the burnt-out lawn

Norman hated the suburbs. The suburbs of Chicago right after World War II were boring and blah. They didn't have the colorful characters, the excitement or, of course, the restaurants, of the city. Norman couldn't mingle with the masses, or meet celebrities, as he could in the city.

He and Phyllis moved to Skokie anyways, a suburb just north of Chicago, a year after they got married in 1951, looking for more space and better schools. They came from the Uptown neighborhood on the city's North Side, part of the great White Flight from many American cities, including Chicago, to the suburbs after World War II.

The Uptown they left in the 1950s was still predominantly White and middle class. They had hoped to raise a family, impossible in their cramped apartment on Ainslie Street, near where Norman grew up, and decided to move on.

So, off to Skokie they went, following other middle-class Jewish families northward.

From the 50s until the end of the 70s, Skokie was a textbook white-picket fence bedroom community. It was all White and, except for a large Jewish population, wasn't ethnic, at all. Immigrants stayed in the city. Other than some Spanish-speaking Mexican busboys and cooks who worked at a few restaurants, the only language spoken in Skokie was English.

The big wave of foreigners bringing many new customs and languages to Skokie were yet to arrive until the 1980s.

There was little entertainment and only a few decent restaurants, like the famous Jewish deli, Kaufman's, and a McDonald's, near each other both on Dempster Street, and the pizza place, Alberti's (now The Village Inn) in downtown Skokie. There were a few hot dog stands like Big Herm's on Dempster. But that was it. If you wanted to see a show – live theater that is, not a movie – or eat a good meal, you had to go into the city.

Norman was a regular on Sunday mornings at Kaufman's but not regular enough to be known. After he left Skokie, he scratched it from his restaurant list. Once when he went without me, he pretended not to speak English, gesturing wildly with his hands, then gently tapping the display case at the goodies he wanted. They fell for the lost foreign tourist trick and filled his order. If I was with him, I'm not sure what I would have done. I probably would have just been quiet, and poker-faced, and let Norman be Norman.

Skokie was also home to Old Orchard, one of the country's first large shopping malls during the mall craze of the 50s. It had top line stores at the time, such as Marshall Field's, a historic Chicago shopping icon, now Macys. Norman was only an occasional shopper, so he didn't care much for Old Orchard, which he lovingly called "Old Ordshit." Norman thought the real Marshall Field's was the main store in downtown Chicago, where he always bought his fancy threads. The one in Skokie didn't meet Norman's fine urban tastes.

He wasn't a real clothes horse, but he had good taste and always seemed to have the right clothes for every occasion and taught me a few things about dressing properly.

The opening of the Edens Expressway in 1951 and the Skokie Swift in 1964 cemented Skokie's ties to the city as a bedroom community, shortening the commute to Norman's office downtown.

I rode on a maiden voyage of the Swift with Norman when it opened, a scared seven-year-old on one of his first train rides, holding on tight to a handrail. I got a commemorative pen with the CTA (Chicago Transit Authority) logo as compensation, a cherished possession I displayed in my bedroom for many years.

Norman became just another foot soldier in the vast army of suburban commuters, schlepping to work downtown every day.

Norman's daily routine wasn't unusual, except for when he shaved every morning. He puffed out his cheeks as he shaved. I didn't understand why, until I asked. I was the typical curious kid fascinated by watching their father shave in the morning. "I can't stand to see my own face in the mirror," Norman used to say. It was just another of Norman's quirky habits I saw growing up.

During the 50s and 60s, Skokie experienced explosive growth as other White urban exiles began flowing in. In those days, Blacks didn't – or rather, couldn't – live in Skokie. They lived in Evanston, the suburb next door to Skokie, which had an old established and thriving Black community. Even after the 1964 civil rights legislation and fair housing legislation in Illinois, plenty of informal barriers kept Blacks out. They would only start arriving with Skokie's immigrant wave in the 80s, when the gates to diversity finally swung open.

To Norman, Skokie was still a wasteland, just a place to stay for the night. Skokie was only a launching pad for raids into the city for restaurants and culture. I, of course, tagged along. As a kid, I was Norman's constant shadow. I got my taste of – and love for – urban life from him.

I always used to say Norman made the ultimate sacrifice for me by moving to Skokie. The main attraction was the schools. I went to Madison Elementary School, built in the 1960s with tall glass windows encircling a lush courtyard. It was sunny and bright with an upbeat atmosphere, a wonderful school for me as a kid. From there, I went to Lincoln Junior High School, just south of downtown Skokie within walking distance of the Ace Hardware, Norman's haunt for his failed home repair projects.

I then went to Niles West High School on Oakton, an award-winning school, which, with Madison and Lincoln, provided me with an excellent primary education. I went to Northwestern University right out of high school and lived in Evanston for a while.

As soon as I finished college and fully moved out, they sold the house and ran back to the city. They couldn't wait to get back.

Norman the Good Neighbor

Norman's dislike for the suburbs didn't change his character. He was still a nice guy and got along with all the neighbors – except for one, Stormy's Father.

He was close with Ralph and Kathleen across the street and Stuart and Norma next door. Both neighbors had daughters my age. Mary and Joan were Ralph and Kathleen's kids, and Marcy and Leslie were Stuart and Norma's daughters. We played together as children on each other's lawns and moved freely between each other's houses.

It was a stereotypical 60s and 70s suburban world. Ralph worked for a large company. Kathleen was a housewife, and Stuart was a surgeon and Norma a nurse. Stuart and Norma had met while working together in a hospital in Hawaii, and they used to come over every Sunday and have a drink with Norman and Phyllis in the back yard.

Norma was cute and petite and, in the warm weather, sometimes wore a tiny bikini when they would come over – at an age when I was starting to notice these things.

Sometimes my father would barbecue. He was a terrible cook. Everything was burnt on the outside and raw on the inside. It got so bad that Phyllis secretly rolled the barbecue into the garbage in the alley when Norman wasn't around.

Norman was heartbroken and asked Phyllis what happened to the barbecue. She fessed up, and Norman went to the local garbage dump in search of his beloved barbecue. Luckily for us, and the neighbors, he never rescued the barbecue and stopped being the neighborhood culinary menace.

Norman's Battle with Stormy's Father

Norman didn't get along with his neighbor on the other side, Ben. Ben was also married with two kids, one of whom had already moved out of the house. There wasn't anything unusual about Ben. He was a typical suburban neighbor, friendly yet quiet, and worked in an office. He wasn't difficult, or abrasive or belligerent. He was just an average guy. Norman still didn't like him.

Due to a clerical error in the property records, Norman and Ben didn't pay their full share of property taxes. The two adjacent houses actually sat on three adjoining lots, not two. Each house sat on its own full lot and then shared a portion of a lot in between. The village only charged each homeowner taxes for their respective full lots, not the shared third lot.

When Ben noticed this, he went to the village to correct the tax bill. Norman was furious. He thought if they were dumb enough to make a mistake, they should pay for it. Ben thought, on the other hand, if he didn't report it, they might end up someday with an astronomical bill for back taxes. Norman understood but still wasn't happy.

Ben had a dog, a sweet golden retriever named Stormy, named for the stormy night he was born. Stormy had white stains on both sides of his mouth from poking his snout through the white picket fence between the two houses.

Norman was so mad at Ben, he stopped talking to him for years. From then on, whenever Ben's name came up, he referred to him only as Stormy's Father.

Norman the Misfit Cub Scout Leader

Though Norman was a good neighbor, he wasn't into the extracurricular group activities common in the suburbs, like Little League or summer camps. He wasn't a joiner. He was too much of a free spirit and too busy with his business. I was a nerd, not a jock. I grew up with girls and never played, or liked, sports, so I never bugged Noman about joining a team or going off to camp. Like Norman, I was allergic to nature and the outdoors.

I was afraid to go near the baseball or the football, or any ball, for that matter, in school gym class. I was the scaredy cat always picked last, if at all, for any team. Fearless and courageous in class – a star pupil – I was a coward on the playing field. I always thought cowards live longer.

Somehow, and it's all a blur to me now, Norman and I became cub scouts. All I remember is one night in a school gym, crowded with screaming boys and eager dads, Norman and I got roped into the local Cub Scout troop. Norman was now the Den Father, and I was one of his Cubs.

Wearing uniforms and tying knots and saying slogans each week in someone's basement just wasn't for us. I think Norman was more interested, anyways, in the Den Mother's tush than leading the troop and, after a year, we were done with scouting.

Norman the Unhandy Man

Norman wasn't handy. He couldn't fix anything. He shouldn't have owned a house. He wasn't cut out for the rigors of homeownership. Repairs? Not in his wheelhouse. It was all part of his anti-suburban chic.

His "workshop" in the basement, if it could be called that, was a disaster. Boxes of mismatched tools were scattered on the floor. I once stepped on a soldering iron he forgot to unplug and burned my ankle. If he needed something, he usually couldn't find it. That is if he even really knew what he was looking for.

Hammers, screwdrivers, whatever, tools were all a mystery to Norman. Anything electrical, or having to be plugged in, like a drill, forget it. They ended up being trophies hung on hooks on perforated boards he unsuccessfully tried to attach to the concrete walls in the basement. Norman still had to buy them, even if he couldn't use them, for bragging rights with neighbors or visitors.

When he didn't know how to operate something, usually the case, he harassed the Ace Hardware on Oakton Street in downtown Skokie with idiotic questions how to use even simple tools. He left them speechless. Some of the things he asked about just couldn't be done. "What if I just attach this to that? Do you have a tool for it?"

If there was a tool, even if he never used it again, he would buy it. Maybe that's why they even still let him back in the store. The Ace survived Norman and is a Skokie retail landmark still in the same spot today on Oakton.

Even screwing in a light bulb, especially if it required a ladder, was a challenge. I saw Norman once putting a ladder over a window outside. I saw him go up the ladder. I saw him fly by the window and fall on the ground. I thought, "Yep, that's my dad trying to fix something again."

Another time, he put a screen door backwards over the back door. Phyllis noticed the door opened inside instead of out and yelled at Norman to fix it. If something didn't fit, Norman would just jam it in harder. It had to work. It just wasn't being forced hard enough.

When Norman finally had to hire somebody, he opted for eccentric over expertise. He wanted to work with likeminded people. Only they understood his craziness. He always knew somebody who knew somebody or had a family member who would do the job.

There was Dave the electrician who was a Holocaust survivor. Skokie, in those days, had the largest population of Holocaust survivors, the reason the Nazis targeted it for their marches in the late 70s. Dave was stubby and sweaty with curly unkempt hair flying around his balding head. He explained in a thick Polish accent how he would fix the power, while he punched holes in the wall to fish wires in.

It was messy and dirty and noisy. Dust swirled around everywhere. Phyllis screamed. The wires made a scraping sound, as if an animal was trapped between the walls. But finally, the lights went on, and all was good again.

Frankenstein in the Basement

My laboratory, next to Norman's chaotic workshop, on the other hand, was neat and organized. It consisted of my chemistry set, small vials of chemicals, test tubes, and beakers, all lined up in tidy rows on metal shelves along the concrete wall. I also had Petri dishes for biology experiments and electronic components for my shortwave radios and Bunsen burners for cooking Frankenstein concoctions.

As long as I didn't burn down, or blow up, the house, or didn't invent a germ to infect the neighborhood, Norman didn't care if Frankenstein himself came up from the basement. Norman took me to local scientific supply stores, typical of Norman always being there for me, whenever I needed more test tubes, equipment, or chemicals, or even just wanted to browse. He bought me whatever I wanted, as long as it was within reason.

In fact, Norman encouraged my crazy experiments. He supported it totally. He thought it was pre-med training for the doctor he hoped I would someday be. Then, like every proud Jewish parent, he could say, "My son, the doctor!"

Norman also encouraged my voracious appetite for books and reading. He dropped me off, whenever I wanted, at Skokie's public library or Kroch's and

Brentano's in Old Orchard, Chicago's famous bookstore chain until it closed in 1995.

"That kid," Norman used to say, "always has his nose in some book."

Norman at War with the Lawn

The inside was only one of Norman's house problems. The outside was another. The houses on the block were a row of neatly manicured lawns except for one with overgrown weeds and knee-high grass burnt to a tantalizing yellow. That was our lawn. It was the knocked-out tooth in an otherwise perfect smile. I didn't realize as a kid that grass was supposed to be green. I always thought the natural color of lawns was supposed to be yellow.

Norman was at war with the lawn. The neighbors didn't complain – at least, not openly – but he knew he had to do something. Finally, he found Quinlan the landscaper. Quinlan smoked a chewed-up cigar, just like Norman, and had short curly hair, also just like Norman, which was probably why Norman liked him. He wore sleeveless muscle t-shirts, barely covering a small pot belly and a small tattoo of an anchor on his shoulder, in the days when only sailors had tattoos.

"I think we can save the lawn," Quinlan told Norman. "But, it'll take some work."

Once a week, Quinlan would bring his crew, day laborers he brought up from Skid Row, to cut the lawn and trim the bushes. The crews were different each week, since they were hung over drunks Quinlan dug up fresh each time. But they did the trick and got the lawn under control, at least, enough to please Norman, and probably secretly, the neighbors.

Norman Hated Pets

Norman hated that other symbol of suburbia: pets. Other neighbors had dogs and cats, like Mary and Joan across the street and Stormy's father next door. Norman was allergic, not physically but mentally, to the idea of an animal in his house.

Norman hated pets – he never had any when he was a kid – and wasn't going to change his mind as an adult. Phyllis, on the other hand, grew up with a dog and had a fondness for pets. She used to tell stories about Dutchess her beloved childhood dog and even showed me photos.

A client of Norman's gave me three gerbils as a gift. He raised them for his kids in a big cage in his house. They were all crammed together and, of course, bred like rabbits. His cage was overflowing, and he gave them away to alleviate overcrowcing.

Phyllis put them in a fish tank converted into a cage with a treadmill and a rectangular can for a makeshift shelter. She threw in cedar chips to absorb the smells from their pee and poop. Norman called them "little rats" and "the little bastards." He couldn't stand the sight of them.

After a few months, one of the gerbils was listless. I pulled it out of the cage and put a stethoscope over its furry tummy. I didn't hear anything. Not that there was much to hear. The stethoscope bell was bigger than the whole gerbil. It was obviously dead. I was depressed.

Even though Norman hated the gerbils, he sympathized with my loss and took me to a forest preserve in Morton Grove, the suburb just west of Skokie, and let me give it a proper burial in the woods.

Within a year, the rest of the "little bastards" died and Norman didn't have to deal with it any more. That was the end of me and pets. Norman was thrilled.

Chadwick the IRS Agent

Now and then, Norman would run into another neighbor, Chadwick. He only saw Chadwick occasionally on the Skokie Swift, on their way to work downtown. Chadwick worked for the IRS, and my father was a CPA. Chadwick wasn't just a normal IRS agent. He was a fraud investigator for the IRS.

As part of his job, Norman often dealt with the IRS and was always scrupulous about his work. He would immediately drop a client who engaged in any impropriety. Still, when Chadwick would see him on the train, he would say, "You know, Dubin, I've been thinking about you," to which Norman would always reply, "Chadwick, please don't think about me."

The New Condo Back to the City

By 1980, I had moved out of the house. Norman and Phyllis were itching to get back into the city and started shopping for condos along the lake.

Three families, all foreigners from the city, looked at their house. One was Cuban, another Indian and the third was Korean. The Korean family fell in love with the house and bought it immediately. It's not a coincidence the shoppers, and ultimate buyer, of my parent's home were all foreigners.

The Anti-Suburbanite

In the 80s, Skokie underwent a tremendous demographic shift. The children of the White Flight crowd were moving out of Skokie, as did their parents, now empty nesters, either back to the city or to suburbs further north and west, many to Buffalo Grove. Foreigners and immigrants poured in from the overcrowded city, as they got a toehold into the middle class.

The foreigners shopping for my parent's home, though not obvious to us at the time, were the cutting-edge of the great Skokie immigrant wave.

As soon as the house sold, Norman and Phyllis left Skokie and never looked back.

And neither did I, that is, until I came back decades later with my wife.

The Skokie of my parents was no longer monochrome and monocultural and monolingual. It had become a multiethnic community. It became the most diverse town in Illinois, earning the name The Ellis Island of The North Shore. It became home to the annual Skokie Festival of Cultures, where a sampling of the ninety languages spoken in Skokie could be heard.

It also became home to nice hotels, fancy restaurants, and outstanding theater. No longer just a sleepy bedroom community, it was now a cultural destination itself.

When Sara and I moved back to Skokie in 2015, I was amazed at the changes. Men in yarmulkes and women in hijabs sat near each other in the public library and shopped at the same stores together.

I walked into a corner market across the street from our new home and was surprised to hear all the customers speaking Russian or Arabic. Foods from Russia and the Middle East were on the shelves. Signs in Russian and Arabic were in other store windows. The many languages I had learned during my travels, I was now using every day just running errands around town.

I sometimes drive by the house where I grew up. I knocked on the door once. A family from Tibet was now living there. It was an "only in Skokie" moment, like the time a mosque took over the space on Main Street where the Holocaust Museum was once located, before it moved to its own more spacious and much fancier building behind Old Orchard.

I never imagined in my wildest dreams Ramadan and Passover and Hanukkah and Christmas would all be celebrated equally side by side in the same community.

The Anti-Suburbanite

I told everybody I had left Skokie to see the world,
and when I came back, the world came to see me.

The Urban Animal

"There's one missing."
-Someone noting the wallpaper in Norman's home bar with drawings of sex positions

The Urban Animal

"Why don't they have a parade for broken down old Jewish CPAs?"
-Norman said after every Chicago parade

Norman was glad, finally, to be back in the city. The prison sentence in Skokie now over, he was released, at last, from custody for serving time as a parent. He was on his home turf, his favorite city, the only city, the city by the lake, one of the five Great Lakes, he always reminded visitors.

Norman could breathe easily again. No more running into the city for art fairs and blues fests on the weekends. No more long trips to his favorite restaurants. No more driving downtown to go shopping at Marshall Field's. And, most importantly, no more lawn overgrown with weeds. The hated lawn in Skokie was now somebody else's problem.

The house in the suburbs was out. The condo in the city was in.

Norman and Phyllis bought a spacious condo on Lake Shore Drive overlooking the lake near Belmont. It was bright and sunny with tall windows extending up to the ceiling and a breathtaking view of Lincoln Park and the boats bobbing up and down in Belmont Harbor.

Norman had a small bar in a closet. At first glance, from a distance, the wallpaper had drawings from an ancient Greek urn. The closet was closed except when Norman got a drink for himself or a guest.

A closer look revealed the drawings were small black figures in various sex positions. They completely covered the wallpaper wall-to-wall.

Someone once told Norman, after staring at the wallpaper in the open closet for a while, "There's one missing."

The Romance of The City

To Norman, the city had a certain romance. His favorite play was Guys and Dolls, the Broadway musical set in New York in the 50s about a bunch of gamblers, smartly dressed in pinstripe suits and fedoras meeting secretly every night in a new location to shoot craps.

Not to be outdone, in Norman's eyes, Chicago had its own colorful history complete with Prohibition-era gangsters gunning each other down on the city's streets. Norman's image of the city, at times, was of Damon Runyon characters on every corner.

Norman was born ten months after the Saint Valentine's massacre in 1929, Chicago's most notorious shootout of alleged bootleggers. By the time he was of age, Prohibition had ended and the rum runners had disappeared. The only Damon Runyon characters left were in Norman's imagination.

Chicago's streets were still full of enough kooky characters, some just grist for his stories and tall tales, others for chatting in the Norman daily talk show.

Besides its gangster past, Chicago was known for its quirky weather, best described as arctic-tropical. It was bitter cold and snowy in the winter and scorchingly hot and humid in the summer. There was never a break. Spring and fall both lasted one day. Spring was a snow storm with icy temperatures one day, followed by 80-degree weather the next day. Then the fall was the reverse, brutally hot one day, then icy rain and sub-zero temperatures the following day.

In the winter, Norman hibernated indoors at the East Bank Club and at his favorite restaurants. He would come home, pound his feet on the doormat, shaking the snow off his shoes, and tell Phyllis and I, "It's colder than a witch's tit out there." I learned about witch's tits as a child from Norman, long before I even knew what tits were.

In the summer, Norman came alive. Besides the restaurants, of course, which put tables outside for the season – like Gibson's and Carmine's overlooking The Viagra Triangle – Norman's other favorite summer haunts were the two swimming pools, one on the upper deck of the East Bank Club and the other at his condo building.

The Swimming Pools:
The Condo and The East Bank Club

Norman was a decent swimmer. He even taught me how to swim as a kid. But swimming wasn't his thing. Just like restaurants weren't about food, pools weren't about swimming. Pools were for socializing. They were places to hang-out, to make new friends or gossip with old ones.

Norman still sometimes took a dip in the condo pool. He would jump in at the deep end then quickly swim over to the shallow side. He might fling his arms over the edge to hang on, kicking the water around for a bit. But, most of the time, he wasn't in the pool. He was walking around and kibbitzing, mixing with his neighbors, the regular crowd who came down to the pool on weekends.

Through the pool, just like every other space Norman inhabited, he got chummy with everybody in the building and who they all liked and, sometimes, didn't like. Norman never ran for the condo board. He wasn't interested. He didn't need to. He already was the big *macher,* Yiddish for a mover and shaker, secretly running the show from the patio.

Norman, of course, was above all that. He wasn't into petty condo politics, or building cliques. He liked, and was liked by, everybody in the building. Norman became the building big shot on the weekends, at least, at the pool. It was probably his margaritas.

If there wasn't a social event, Norman would create one, spur of the moment just for the occasion. Norman was famous for one thing at the pool – his margaritas. He could be counted on to make his unique concoction for everybody. He brought his little mixing kit and pitcher with liquor and ingredients down to the pool every weekend.

People tended to stay in Norman's condo building for many years. There was low turnover. Norman stayed there until he passed and Phyllis until she had to go to a nursing home.

"The only place people move to after being in this building," said Carl, one of Norman's neighbors, "is either Florida or Piser's." Piser was a chain of Jewish funeral homes in Chicago.

Norman brought his suburban tradition – the drink in the backyard with the neighbors – to the city. Except in the city the backyard became the pool deck and the neighbors were his fellow condo dwellers.

Norman wasn't a big drinker.   When he drank, it was always just one small glass. He drank only to be social. That was it. He never drank to excess, and I never saw him drunk.

His obligatory Kettle One, known by every waiter at every restaurant, was his only indulgence. Every waiter had to know about Norman's Kettle One. They might be tested later. Not knowing Norman's favorite drink, well, just wouldn't look good. No one wanted to be left out of The Golden Tipper's Club.

Norman and Phyllis's condo was on Lake Shore Drive, the city's elegant lakefront expressway running from Hollywood Avenue on the North Side through Jackson Park, ending at Marquette Drive and Jeffrey Drive on the South Side, connecting two iconic neighborhoods, Edgewater on the north and South Shore to the south, and everything else in between.

The "Drive," as it was known to the natives, lined by the trees of Lincoln Park on one side and a wall of high-rise apartments and condos on the other, looked more like an elegant boulevard in Europe than a major urban artery in a city in the American Midwest. From North Avenue to Oak Street, the Drive ran along the beach, past people playing volleyball.

The condo was strategically located near Belmont Avenue on the North Side next to Chicago's biggest summer attraction, its expansive street fairs, another of Norman's favorite pastimes. Whole blocks were lined with food booths and people selling their wares in outdoor markets.

Norman especially loved the art fairs. His favorites were in Old Town and the Gold Coast. He would chat with artists and sound like a real art aficionado. He could people watch, have a snack or two and, as always happened, run into an old friend, or someone else he knew.

Norman took me often to Starks Warehouse, which used to be on Canal Street, not far from Manny's. He loved to look at all the discount goods. Starks sold every imaginable household item. He explained it was railroad salvage, when a rail car tipped over and a store didn't want the merchandise anymore, they would unload it for cheap at Starks.

Norman also took the whole family every June to the Gay Pride Parade along Broadway, a few blocks walk just west of the condo. He loved the pageantry and dressed up characters.

"Everybody in this town gets a parade," Norman always said afterward. "Why don't they have a parade for broken down old Jewish CPAs like me?"

Norman loved blues and jazz music and went like clockwork every summer to the Chicago Blues Festival in Grant Park.

Also in Grant Park, Norman went religiously every summer to the Tastes of Chicago. The "Taste," as the locals call it, is the city's premiere foodie event with booths and food trucks from at least four dozen restaurants and food vendors. Even Norman's favorite lunch place, Manny's, was there.

After Norman was done making the rounds at the Taste, he would make a care package, usually with juicy ribs, and hand deliver it to a paraplegic friend, who was housebound in a condo on Rush Street.

Norman could be incredibly thoughtful and generous with his friends. He was always there, his heart and his hand open, for someone in need, whether to bring food, or just visit a lonely friend at home or in the hospital. He once even bought ribs for all the guys who worked in the condo garage. No reason. No special occasion. Just like that – a spontaneous act of kindness.

Norman never forgot to send us a box of steaks every year for Christmas. He never told us they were coming. They would just show up at the house.

A waitress told Norman and Phyllis she had missed her train after work. Norman eagerly offered to give her a ride home. It was just Norman being Norman again, always willing to help. It turned out she lived in a distant suburb. Norman happily made the long trip without a peep. Phyllis was seething but kept quiet the whole trip. On the way back, she let loose and let Norman have it. She yelled at him the whole way back.

The East Bank Club

Then there was Norman's second home, the East Bank Club.

Norman went there almost every day after work. Racquetball ball was his daily passion. You couldn't miss him on the court. He wore an eye guard, unlike other players, after he almost lost an eye when a ball hit him in the face. The eye guard was his signature from when he started playing in the 1970s at another club and was still learning the game.

Norman was in incredible shape. Other than chewing his cigar, he had good health habits and was health conscious. He watched his weight, never getting a gut in middle age, and always followed his doctor's instructions. He played racquetball at the East Bank until he was eighty years old.

Norman's locker was next to a homicide detective, who wore a t-shirt, "Our day begins, when your day ends." Norman thought it was funny and talked about it all the time. From the way he talked, I thought he knew some famous on-screen detective.

Between the bar, the restaurant and the grill, Norman met plenty of other famous people at the club. Norman was even on a first name basis with the founder and CEO of the East Bank Club, Dan Levin, also a major Chicago real estate developer.

Norman, of course, had met Obama, presumably, at some point, with his clothes on, and Jesse Jackson, sweaty after his workout and with a towel over his shoulders, who warmly fist bumped Norman every time they met, as if they were old buddies.

He also would have a drink at the bar with Lou Holland, a well-known investment manager, and introduced me once to Saul Bellow, the Nobel prize-winning author, when he lived in Chicago many years ago.

Norman saw Oprah Winfrey several times at the club. Unlike other lesser-known celebrities, she would arrive in the front lobby surrounded by a half dozen or so body guards. She was dressed in her sweats with no makeup and had a serious look on her face like she was ready to work out. Norman didn't mess with Oprah. He couldn't even get near her.

Then, just like his other favorite restaurants, the East Bank had its share of Mexican waiters and waitresses, all students of Norman's class in Broken Yiddish.

Norman met countless people through the East Bank as he made his daily rounds from the racquetball court to the restaurants and up to the pool deck. Norman didn't miss a single corner of the club.

Not A Country Gentleman

When Norman was in Chicago, he rarely set foot outside the city. He was the consummate urban animal. A true city dweller, he hated the Great Outdoors. To Norman, the outdoors meant walking in Lincoln Park across from his condo, or walking at a street fair.

Real nature with woods and prairies or big open farmland, wasn't Norman's thing, at all. Nature was something hostile, and to be feared and avoided at all costs. He took us one summer to Door County in rural Wisconsin, a popular vacation spot with Chicagoans. We stayed in a cabin and went bike riding on lonely two-lane country roads.

The country was beautiful and the air was fresh. It wasn't for Norman. After only a few days, he was itching to get back to the bright lights of the city. The diners and small-town restaurants couldn't match up to Norman's haunts back in Chicago.

Besides, Norman didn't know anyone in Door County. Friendly and warm, the locals were still strangers, and Norman couldn't stand being in a place where he was an unknown.

Phyllis wasn't happy either. She complained the whole trip, about the cabin and the food, and yelled at Norman incessantly. It wasn't much of a vacation for him.

Norman couldn't wait to get back to Chicago. The East Bank Club awaited him with one big draw – its women.

The Don Juan

"I couldn't have a mistress in this town.
Everybody knows me."
-Norman

The Don Juan

"After she finished with me, there would be nothing left but teeth and hair."
-Norman about being with a younger woman

Norman loved women. If he saw a pretty woman in the distance, he would comment under his breath, usually in lewd or inappropriate language. For a long time, I wondered if he had some secret mistress on the side.

"I couldn't have a mistress in this town," Norman used to say. "I couldn't take her anywhere. Everybody knows me."

The answer came when I opened Norman's will. I breathed a sigh of relief. I had no secret half-siblings. In the end, Norman was all talk. He had no secret mistresses or other girlfriends on the side. He was completely devoted and faithful to Phyllis.

I still pictured Norman, if he had outlived Phyllis, as the 80-year-old guy marrying a 25-year-old bimbo he met at the East Bank Club. I couldn't imagine what would have happened. Fortunately, I didn't have to.

"After she finished with me," Norman would say about a woman too young for him to handle. "There would be nothing left but teeth and hair."

Norman's two loves at the East Bank Club were racquetball and girl watching, and the club was a garden full of temptation and earthly delights – for his eyes.

Once, when I was with Norman at the club, the grill on the second floor was booked up. We waited on the first floor and couldn't get a table there either. Norman was about to leave, when he looked up and saw a slinky young woman in tight leotards come down the stairs.

 "On second thought," Norman turned and looked at me, "Let's stay here."

Norman always complained he missed the sexual revolution of the 1960s. He was already married to Phyllis over a decade before the revolution's first shots were fired. I didn't want to know what went on in their bedroom, but I gathered it wasn't a revolution. Besides, from what I heard from those who lived through it and survived – I was too young to experience it – Norman didn't miss much anyways.

Norman, The Mismatchmaker

Since Norman could only look, but not touch, any of the beauties he met at the East Bank Club, he lived his fantasies through me, sending his stable my way before I was married. When Norman called, with some new name and number, I never knew what would come through the door.

They were all disasters.

There was the sexy little school teacher who kept telling me she really wanted to date a lawyer. One day, a lawyer magically appeared on her door step, and not surprisingly, she dumped me and was gone. There was the cute obstetrician who squeezed me in between baby deliveries, until she met another doctor who fit better into her schedule.

There was the woman in an itsy bitsy teenie weenie string bikini at the East Bank Club pool visiting from Europe. How Norman charmed her phone number out of her, I'll never know. I couldn't get back to her for a couple of days. Meanwhile, Norman called me umpteen times to check in. "Did you call her yet?" "No, not yet," I said. Do you want to call her?" He stopped asking. It didn't matter. It never went anywhere. A few dates later, she went back to her boyfriend in Europe and forgot all about me.

There was the daughter of a real estate developer who was a foot and half taller than me and had a floor-length fur coat that smothered me. I felt like I was talking to her chest. She felt like she was talking to the top of my head. She said she already had a boyfriend but wasn't happy and was shopping around. That didn't go anywhere either.

Outside the club, there was the Russian Jewish cutie pie, who Norman met on the street with her parents in Rogers Park, a neighborhood on the North Side home to many recent Russian Jewish immigrants in the 1970s. Norman arranged for us to meet her and her family in their modest apartment.

She had just arrived from the Soviet Union a few days before. She didn't speak a word of English. Her father had to be the interpreter. It was awkward. What was Norman thinking?

It would be a few more decades before I would move to Skokie and learn Russian to deal with my new neighbors, some of whom had arrived from the ex-Soviet Jewish enclave in Rogers Park.

The Dinner Babes

Beyond, the East Bank Club, Norman went to some annual dinners for his business, where he couldn't stop talking about the women, and how they dressed up. There was the Italian bank client with the bankers and their wives. "You wouldn't believe

how high the slits were on their skirts," he said.
"Those Italian women were all so sexy."

Then there was the annual Chicago Urban League
Gala, a black-tie affair, attended by all the top
power brokers in the city's Black community. They
raised money for scholarships for Black students
and organizations. Norman's company bought a
table, and he went with Phyllis every year. He
never mentioned the league's charitable activities.
All he could talk about the next day was the pretty
women and their sexy outfits.

The Politically Incorrect Norman

Norman came from an era when men said
whatever they wanted to women and could get
away with it. Though he never meant to offend or
harass, he said some things to women that would
get him into trouble today. He wasn't always what
would could be called, by today's standards,
politically correct.

Norman told the wife of a close friend of mine,
after meeting her the first time, "You're one hell of
a sexy broad." The word "broad" came from what
decade? I didn't want to know.

Norman was in the elevator of his condo building,
when a young father stepped on with his infant

daughter, maybe two or three years old, perched on his shoulder. With her curly hair and rosy cheeks, she was adorable. She looked right at Norman. Norman looked right back. "Buy me, do me, take me," he said. She smiled and giggled and clapped her little hands. I don't know if she understood. I just rolled my eyes.

Norman's comments ranged from the flaky to the rude.

The flaky: "She has a low-slung ass." I didn't ask. I didn't want to know.

The rude: "If you get up in the morning, and it's as stiff as a bored. You won't fall out of bed. You'll be OK."

Then there was the plain bizarre, women with too much makeup or overdressed, who Norman just called "*tchotchkes*," Yiddish for a trinket or bangle.

Norman always behaved himself in his office. No flirting. No staring or ogling. No off-the-wall dirty comments. But sometimes he wasn't sure. Now and then, he would check in with HR and ask "How am I doing?" The answer was always the same. He was fine.

The Don Juan

When Norman saw a story in the news about a prostitution bust, he used to say, "How are those ladies going to make a living now?"

It reminded Norman of a scene from his favorite movie, The Last Detail, about two sailors, one played by Jack Nicholson, escorting a young Navy guy to the brig for a long prison sentence for a minor offense. They decide to show him a good time, getting him drunk and laid along the way.

In one scene, the two sailors are sitting on a sofa in the front room of a brothel as women in slinky lingerie walk back and forth with their customers. They're telling each other old sailor stories, as if it was a normal day at sea, while their boy is in some room doing his business. Norman thought the scene was hilarious.

The End of the Norman Dating Service

Norman stopped fixing me up on dates, when I met Sara – not through the East Bank Club – who I eventually married.

After I proposed, we held a dinner celebrating our engagement with only our parents at the Oak Room in the Drake Hotel on Michigan Avenue. It was also the first time Norman and Phyllis met Sara's parents, Sid and Eleanor.

Everything went fine. The parents all hit it off. How couldn't they? They were also obviously Jewish – Norman didn't have to ask – and that was all that mattered.

Then Sara and I brought up the wedding. The four parents suddenly started talking over us and pushed us aside, planning the wedding, as if we weren't even there. Sara and I lost control of our own wedding. The parents had taken over. It was now their show, not ours.

Norman was on his best behavior. He didn't make any off-color jokes or point at any hot babes in the restaurant.

He wanted to make an impression on the in-laws to be. Little did they know what was to come.

As Norman was leaving, he spotted Jack O'Malley, then Cook County State's Attorney and went up to him. "Hey, You're the State's Attorney, right?" Norman asked, handing him a business card. "Thank you, Mr. Dubin," O'Malley responded confidently, as if he was on the campaign trail. He put the card in the front pocket of his shirt. "I'm going to add you to our donor list."

The Don Juan

Norman frantically tried to grab the card out of O'Malley's pocket, but not in time for O'Malley to turn and walk away.

Sara and I got married six months later on July 4 at The Knickerbocker Hotel down the street. I tell people, in true Norman style, there are fireworks on our anniversary even if I do nothing.

That was over thirty years ago, and we've been happily married ever since. Norman and Phyllis lovingly took Sara in with open arms to be with me on The Norman and Phyllis Show.

The Great Orator

"I picked up the wrong kid in the hospital."
-Norman said when I spoke Spanish

The Great Orator

*"I don't know where that kid picks it up.
I never leave him out of my sight for a minute."
-Norman when I was picking my nose*

I always looked to Norman for advice. I thought he was a sage, maybe even some great undiscovered scholar. I should have known better.

I knew I was in trouble as soon as Norman would say "that kid." He wouldn't call me by my name. He would just call me "that kid." Those two words were an ominous sign the oracle was about to speak. I knew a great life lesson, from Norman's world, was about to be issued from the mountain.

When Norman saw me picking my nose, he would grace me with this bit of wisdom. First, he would put his finger in his nose. Then, he would say, "I don't know where that kid picks it up. I never leave him out of my sight for a minute."

When Norman heard me swear or use foul language, he would say, "I sent that kid to Northwestern and Columbia. I don't know where he picked up that kind of language."

When Norman heard me speaking Spanish with his buddies, the Mexican waiters, he would say, "I picked up the wrong kid in the hospital."

The Great Orator

I had a habit as a kid of looking down and not speaking clearly. "Stand up straight," Norman used to say. "Stop mumbling. I can't hear you."

I also looked to Norman for advice on buying clothes. He had very good taste. He was always perfectly dressed, perfectly put together, his kerchief, matching his tie, neatly folded in the front pocket of his suit.

Norman used to buy his shirts at Brooks Brothers in the Loop. Sometimes he would take me with him to buy shirts. His sales guy, Diego from Cuba, had an eagle eye. He didn't need a measuring tape. He figured out my measurements just by looking at me.

Later, when I would wear one of the shirts he had bought for me, he would say, "That's a nice shirt. Where did you get it?"

The secret to Norman's brilliance was only revealed after he died. I found a copy of the book, The 776 Stupidest Things Ever Said, under a pile of papers on his desk, next to the stinky glass ashtray where he used to put his soggy cigar stub. I was deflated. My image of the great scholar was shattered.

I finally realized that book was where he got some of his wackiest sayings. It was the book of books, perfect for pseudo intellectuals, like Norman, a self-help guide for the hopelessly inarticulate.

Otherwise, Norman wasn't much of a reader. He didn't have a lot of books on the shelf, except for one that stood out – a paperback copy of Machiavelli's The Prince. Based on how he conducted himself in business and with people, in general, I don't think he ever read it.

I often wondered if his other inspiration was Mayor Richard J. Daley, the first of the father-and-son dynasty who led Chicago from 1956 until his death in 1976. Daley the elder was known for saying some crazy stuff.

"The police are not here to create disorder," Daley famously said on live TV during the riots at the 1968 Democratic convention. "The police are here to preserve disorder." I saw those riots and Daley's comment live on TV from our den in Skokie.

Norman simply couldn't verbally express himself. Words weren't his friends. Norman wasn't a great orator or an eloquent speaker. He often got tongue tied on the simplest words and phrases. He was incredibly inarticulate. He didn't have a speech impediment. He simply couldn't communicate. He couldn't put a sentence together.

I never really knew why. It couldn't have come from his family. His mother, Grandma Ida, and the rest of his family, even his Grandpa Ike who had a heavy Yiddish accent all his life, all seemed to be able to speak just fine. Who knows? Maybe Grandma Ida nagged him speechless as a child.

Yet, amazingly, people still seemed – most of the time – to understand him.

I joked with Norman, when I was "that kid," he needed to take remedial English classes. I said he should take English as a First Language, my adaptation of the English as a Second Language classes taken by English learners, or maybe another course I made up entitled English for Native Speakers of English.

The Infamous "Klinsky" Router

Once Norman misnamed something, the incorrect name stuck.

Norman had a special name for the Linksys router he used for his computers at home – "The Klinsky." He first announced this to the world at a family dinner at an upscale French restaurant in River North in Chicago. My brother-in-law, Jeremy, and his wife, Lisa, were in town from San Diego. Jeremy was an electrical and computer engineer and an executive at a small tech company. Jeremy knew routers.

When Norman said the Klinsky wasn't working, we all looked at each other. I turned to Jeremy, asking if he knew about a router made in Poland. It took us a minute. Then, we figured out, he was talking about his Linksys router at home.

Thus, it was said. Henceforth, the Linksys was to be known as the Klinsky. "Hey, dad, how's the Klinsky working today?" I would ask.

I once worked at a company called Trustwave. For some unknown reason, Norman called it, "True Eyes." I have no idea where he got that, or where it came from. Once he got True Eyes in his head, he never let it go. I always had to tell him I was doing fine in my job at True Eyes.

Norman had a fascination with computers later in life. Personal computers weren't available until he was well over sixty years old. Yet, though he never got the names of the parts right, like the Klinsky, he became proficient enough to do his accounting work. He was able to use accounting software, and Excel spreadsheets and Word documents and navigate around the Web, even to find pornography, which I found on his laptop after he died.

Norman would go to computer stores to buy parts and software. He said the stores were "where the nerds herd," and he called the staff, "way-out eggheads."

Norman had other pithy – and short – pieces of advice.

When I asked him about in-laws, his answer, "Marry an orphan." When I asked him about long-term disability insurance, he said, "Die young." There were just things I learned never to ask Norman.

When he talked about being a father, Norman used to say, "I was only involved in this for a few minutes before you were born." Then he would add, "After that, you're on your own, kid."

The British Are Coming!

The first time we went to the UK, when I was a kid, was to see Norman's childhood neighbor David. Norman found the British accent both charming and amusing. London had plenty of its own eccentric characters in trench coats and bowler hats, all carrying the obligatory umbrella for misty London, to keep Norman busy.

The Great Orator

Norman could pierce even the stodgy British reserve. He didn't let it stop him from trying to break the ice. Everybody was more than willing to chat, including the lonely old gentleman wearing a bowler hat and carrying an umbrella, who sat across from us on the Tube one Sunday afternoon. He heard Norman's American accent and just started talking with the friendly Yank from across the Pond.

Norman was in stitches when someone on a double-decker bus told him he was going to "buy a lot and shove up a house." When he heard "rain improving to fog" in a weather report, he roared. When he heard a cricket match on the radio, he put his finger in his mouth and pulled it out gradually, making a popping sound, imitating the slow pitch, which Norman thought was as boring as hell.

London had plenty of "birds" in hot pants, the short shorts fashionable on Carnaby Street in the 1970s, to rival any girl watching opportunities Norman had back in Chicago.

Then there were the tall tales. . .

Norman never let the truth get in the way of a good story.

Norman told everybody, "We have family who fought on both sides of the Civil War." Well, while we had cousins in the South, our first ancestors arrived in the 1880s, fifteen years after the Civil War ended.

Along the same timeline, Norman said, "Your Grandma Brandy saw the Chicago Fire." No way. She didn't arrive in Chicago until 1883, a full ten years after the Great Fire.

Then there were more myths about our "Confederate" relatives. Norman told me the cousins in Arkansas, the only Jewish family in Osceola, had an Antebellum mansion with their characteristic tall columns.

When Sara and I got there, it was a simple one-story ranch. They had either removed the columns, or sold the mansion sometime after the Civil War, presumably. I didn't ask. I didn't have to.

The same family had a daughter who participated in beauty pageants in Arkansas. Norman said, "Your cousin was a runner-up for Miss Arkansas." Nope. She was a runner up in a regional beauty pageant. She had, in fact, won many awards – and we saw the trophies to prove it – for beauty pageants, but not for Miss Arkansas.

Then, Norman bragged about my achievements. He was my best spokesperson, even if he didn't get his facts straight.

"That kid speaks fourteen dialects of Arabic," Norman said. I only, in fact, speak three.

"That kid was the Westinghouse Award winner," Norman told everybody when I went to Washington as one of the forty finalists for the prestigious national science award in 1975. That was as far as I went. I wasn't "the winner" or one of the top ten finalists.

Then there was my uncle the war hero. Not exactly. Norman screwed that up too. My Uncle Ronnie did, in fact, have a stunningly successful career in the Judge Advocate Corp (JAG) in the Navy. He retired at the rank of Captain, just a breath away from Admiral.

Of course, Norman told everybody, "My brother-in-law the Admiral." It seemed Norman gave Ronnie a promotion every time somebody asked. "Has he made me Secretary of Defense yet," Ronnie asked me. "Not yet," I said. "But you know that's coming."

The Jewish Guy

"Isn't everybody Jewish?"
-Norman

The Jewish Guy

"I'm a Galitzianer!"
-Norman describing his Jewish tribe

Norman thought everybody was Jewish until proven innocent. When someone surprised Norman by not being Jewish, Norman made sure they, at least, knew he was Jewish.

Norman wanted the world to know he was Jewish, whether through his license plate, MAZLTOV, or the dozens of expressions he spouted in public in Yiddish, a language he didn't really speak but often abused and mispronounced. Sometimes, I think, some of the sayings Norman claimed as Yiddish were just gibberish he made up.

Even with weighty matters like his own Jewish identity and religion, he never took himself too seriously. Born and raised in a diverse city like Chicago, he knew enough about other people, and their religions, to be able to make stupid – though harmless – comments. Norman was a one-man show – his mission to entertain, not offend. He may have flown stuff off the top of his head otherwise, but when it came to people's identities and religions, he spoke carefully and knew what was off-limits.

"You know, I don't eat meat either on Fridays during Lent," Norman once told a Catholic priest. "Just in case one of us is wrong."

That priest was on the board of DePaul University in Chicago, the Catholic college Norman attended, and where, presumably, he must have learned something about the religion – or at least about Lent's dietary rules. Norman eventually served on DePaul's board.

That priest walked into Gene & Georgetti once on a busy Saturday night. He spotted Norman and burst out laughing. He came over to the table and hugged Norman. Apparently, Norman was a real hit on the board, since the priest couldn't stop praising him up and down for his great work, which apparently didn't include teaching broken Yiddish to other priests on the board, who, like Mexican waiters, would normally have been fodder for Norman's language lessons.

Norman assumed everybody understood what he meant when he told people he was a "*Galitzianer*."

If someone didn't know what a *Galitzianer* was – usually the case, especially among *Goyim*, or Gentiles – or didn't understand some other obscure piece of Jewish culture, Norman, of course, was there to explain. Norman was a Jewish culture ambassador, for the culture of a religion not known for being missionary.

When Norman said the word *Galitzianer*, he might have had some blank stares. But when he brought up Alexander Hamilton, everybody knew who he was talking about. Hamilton was one of our Founding Fathers. When the Broadway play Hamilton came out in 2015, Norman added another minor Jewish factoid to his repertoire. This was, of course, after the bank robber introduction.

"You know Alexander Hamilton and I have something in common," Norman started telling people. "We both had a Jewish mother." Norman made it a point to tell everyone Hamilton's mother was Jewish, an obscure detail often overlooked in his bio. As an adult, Hamilton didn't practice Judaism, or claim to be Jewish. But, as a child, his mother sent him to a Jewish school where he studied Torah and Hebrew.

Norman wasn't just a cultural Jew, as many non-observant Jews describe themselves. He was still God-fearing and firmly believed in the Jewish religion, even if he couldn't articulate its theological fine points. Fortunately, he never had to. Nobody ever asked. They knew better.

Norman was like many Jews of his generation, children of deeply Orthodox immigrants, who became far less religious than their parents for a variety of reasons. It was better, in their mind, to hide being Jewish in the new country. Usually, it was just the desire to blend into American society. Often, it was also a reaction to antisemitism they encountered moving into a new, and sometimes scary, non-Jewish world.

Still, though wild and woolly in the late 1800s and early 1900s, American cities weren't as dangerous as the *shtetls* of the old country, where a Jew could end up dead or, at least, severely beaten for making the wrong move. Those memories stuck hard with Jewish immigrants, who brought them to America. It made them keep up their guard even in the relative safety of their new adopted home.

Norman's family lost its Kosher credentials early on after arriving in Chicago. Sholom, his immigrant great grandfather, was strictly Orthodox. By the time his daughter, Grandma Brandy married Ike in 1903, no trace of Orthodox garb can be seen in their wedding photo. No *sheitel* for Grandma Brandy, the traditional wig worn by observant Jewish women to hide their hair. She looked like any other young American woman in the early 1900s with a flowing skirt.

Ike also appeared to have abandoned Orthodoxy. I never saw any photo of him, from his wedding onward, with a *yarmulke*, the obligatory Jewish skullcap.

Grandma Ida was non-observant like her parents, Ike and Celia. But she was a member of the local Conservative synagogue, Anshei Emet, in Chicago's Uptown neighborhood, where Norman had his bar mitzvah in 1943. Anshei Emet is still active to this day and is one of Chicago's oldest synagogues, founded in 1873. Norman returned to his childhood synagogue, when he moved back into the city in 1980.

The Twice-A-Year Jew

When Norman returned to Anshei Emet, he wasn't any more active the second time around. He was still just a Twice-A-Year Jew, the term for Jews who only go to synagogue on the High Holidays: Rosh Hashana, the Jewish New Year, and Yom Kippur, the Day of Atonement ten days later.

Norman felt it was still extremely important to go to synagogue even if only on Rosh Hashana and Yom Kippur. As soon as I was old enough, around ten years old, he and Phyllis started taking me to services at their local synagogue in Skokie, Temple Judea. When I asked him why, he always just said, "It's important. That's it." When I pushed him for an explanation, he wouldn't answer. It was just one of those Normanisms I had to accept.

During the Yom Kippur service, there is a prayer, called *Al Chet*, meaning "sin" in Hebrew, listing sins for which we should ask forgiveness. Norman always looked down on me with a scowl, when the sin of disrespecting parents came up. He would look right into my eyes and say loudly, *"Al Chet – for the sin we have sinned against You by not honoring our parents."*

Norman wanted to make sure I heard that clearly. I found it odd, since I always respected my father. I was a good kid and not a problem, or rebellious, child in any way. A mad scientist, yes, who drove both my parents nuts with all my crazy projects, but a difficult child, no. Now and then, I have to admit sometimes I could be an obnoxious brat, maybe even a smart mouth. But then, how couldn't I, growing up and living with Norman?

Or Maybe the Three-Times-A-Year Jew

Maybe it would be more accurate to call Norman a Three-Times-A-Year Jew. His favorite holiday was Passover. Norman shined during Passover. It wasn't about being religious. The whole escape from Egypt thing was secondary. It was about showing off his hospitality and generosity. He was

the big *macher*, a big shot, to his friends and family.
Norman owned Passover. Nobody else in the
family came close.

He would reserve a huge square table at the East
Bank Club, right in the front corner near the
entrance, where everybody could see. He hosted
at least three or four dozen people – and paid the
bill for the entire crew. There was family, people
from his condo building, old friends, like Angelo
and Olga, long lost cousins and their spouses and
kids. It was a madhouse. People all talked over
each other and ignored the brief Seder. It was just
like Norman loved it.

There was a straggler once, someone visiting from
my company's office in Brazil, who I just couldn't let
sit alone in the hotel that night. He was an avowed
Seventh Day Adventist, who asked if we served
pork at the Seder. He wanted to make sure we
weren't breaking his dietary restrictions. Of course
not, I told him. We're Jewish. No worries. No pork
at even Norman's less than kosher Seder.

The Haggadah, the traditional prayer book just for
Seder? Way too long for Norman's taste. No hours
of prayers before the meal even started. His guests
were hungry, waiting for that delicious brisket
being sliced in the other room. It was on Norman's
tab. He was the king. He had to be in charge.

Norman chopped the Haggadah down to the basics, the Four Questions, and the Ten Plagues. That was it. Maybe a half hour – tops. The Seder was done. Norman's speed version.

Norman loved reciting the Ten Plagues out loud, where the tradition is to dip your finger in a glass of wine whenever a plague was mentioned, and then tap the drop of wine on your plate each time.

The height of the evening was Norman singing *Chad Gadya* after dinner. It was a real treat to see Norman singing out at the top of his lungs. *Chad Gadya* is like a Jewish version of the Twelve Days of Christmas. It starts as a story about a father buying a goat for his son for two *zuzim*, some long-forgotten ancient currency, then builds up from there.

From there, the goat gets eaten by a cat, and then a dog bites the cat, and then a stick beats the dog, and then a fire burns the stick – and to make a long story short – after some bloody encounters with an ox, a butcher, and the Angel of Death, the Holy One swoops down and makes the world right again.

Norman mumbled his way through the song, the only words I could clearly make out were "*Chad Gadya*" and "two *zuzim*" at the end of each chorus.

As for the other holidays, the only one that mattered to Norman and Phyllis was Hanukkah. They always gave me a gift on the first, and only on the first night, not any other night. It was just one gift for the whole eight days of the holiday. It was usually either a book or some electronic gadget I had wanted. Pretty simple, but still thoughtful and loving.

Norman Gave Me a Jewish Education

Norman made sure I had a decent Jewish education. He enrolled me in Hebrew school at Temple Judea in Skokie when I was ten years old. I went two nights a week and a half day on Saturday morning. It was grueling after a long day at public school.

I attended until I was in high school well after my bar mitzvah, unusual for most suburban Jewish kids, who usually drop out right after their bar mitzvah.

At a Purim carnival during Hebrew school one year, there was a booth with rows of tiny bowls, each with a single goldfish. I tossed a ping pong ball. It landed in one of those tiny bowls. I won the prize – a plastic bag with a little goldfish. In honor of the occasion, I named the fish "Purim."

The Jewish Guy

I proudly took Purim home to Norman and Phyllis. As expected, since Norman hated pets, he ignored it. Phyllis jumped in to help.

Phyllis found a small bowl for the fish and put it on my dresser. Sadly, the next morning, I saw Purim floating on top of the water. He had died overnight. I was heartbroken.

Phyllis felt sorry for me and took me to the pet store in downtown Skokie the next day to buy a new goldfish and a real fish tank complete with an electronic pump and filter. While waiting at the store, I leaned against a tank with a huge nasty looking fish, where my finger was dangling in the water. The store clerk came over and scared the daylights out of me.

"Take your finger out of that tank," he quietly scolded me. "That's a piranha. They're a deadly fish from the Amazon. They can eat a whole cow in thirty minutes." I flinched and jerked my finger out of the water. I was shaken the rest of the day. I couldn't get the image out of my mind of a whole cow being eaten by a bunch of angry fish. I felt lucky my finger was still intact.

The new goldfish didn't last long either, only three weeks, despite Phyllis's diligent care. She made sure to keep the tank clean and regularly refreshed the water. It didn't help. I wasn't meant to take care of animals – or fish either. That was the end of pets for me – until I got gerbils years later.

Norman Teaches Me About Antisemitism

I only figured out when I was older why Norman's jovial Jewish nature was just a cover. It hid his own personal brushes with antisemitism long before I was on the scene.

Norman grew up and lived in an era when antisemitism was widespread. Most companies didn't hire Jews. Whole neighborhoods and country clubs were off limits. Restrictions, even if invisible or unspoken, were everywhere – hotels, restaurants, and private grammar schools.

Jews weren't welcome at many resorts either. Norman used to go as a kid in the 1930s with Grandma Ida to Michigan. Most vacation spots in Wisconsin, closer and more accessible to Chicago, were "restricted," the euphemism of the day for places closed to Jews. The families of his childhood Jewish friends also frequented communities like South Haven, where a Star of David looking down from the steeple was the only way to tell the small building on the main drag, which looked like a one-room church, was really a synagogue.

Even Potsy Pearl, a reputed Jewish mobster from Chicago, according to Norman, could only vacation in Michigan. Norman told me how he saw Pearl once stroll right past him on a nearby beach surrounded by body guards with pistols in holsters. Of course, with Norman, I never really knew if it was just another tall tale or the memory of an impressionable child.

Norman entered the work force at a time when most companies didn't hire Jews. He had graduated from DePaul with a degree in accounting and tax law. Professional firms, even in law and accounting, often barred Jews. Jewish professionals formed their own parallel firms, safe havens from the Gentile firms rejecting them, where their brethren could find work.

Norman ended up starting his own two-man accounting practice in the 1950s with another Jewish accountant. Their clients were mostly Jewish. They were together until their business grew to the point where they had to merge with a larger accounting firm in the 1980s.

Those who weren't professionals started their own businesses. Some went into real estate, an entrepreneurial business with no ethnic or religious barriers to entry. Others went into consumer and industrial product niches. Many, after struggling for years, often built wildly successful businesses.

The Jewish Guy

They ended up better off than had they tried to climb a corporate ladder non-existent for Jews.

Norman's experiences with antisemitism were always just under the surface, and his stories came out when least expected.

Norman had bittersweet feelings about me going to Northwestern University in Evanston. Not because it competed with his beloved DePaul. He was proud I was able to get into such a prestigious school.

Norman was upset about the strict Jewish quota in his day at Northwestern. He, like other Jewish kids his age, couldn't get admitted. Northwestern, at the time, was effectively closed to most Jewish students. Norman had only one Jewish friend, he could remember, who managed to get in under the quota.

Apparently, I learned when I got older, the quota extended to other ethnic groups. Some of Angelo's friends, Norman's childhood neighbor and lifelong friend, who was Greek, told me stories about also being denied admission to Northwestern because they were Greek.

The Jewish quota, at least, was gone by the time I arrived at Northwestern in the late 1970s. The story goes, according to Norman, the Crown family, a wealthy Jewish family in Chicago, funded construction of the modernistic administration building and clock tower with its namesake in downtown Evanston in 1968 in exchange for Northwestern dropping its Jewish quota.

Norman brought the subject up often. He eventually got over it. His pride over me as a Northwestern grad was greater than his anger over the quota. He just didn't want me to forget he couldn't go there.

By the time I was around, the official barriers – at least, on the surface – came down after the Civil Rights Act of 1964, which barred discrimination, among other things, on religion and ethnicity.

I didn't experience antisemitism as a child, since I was only seven years old in 1964. My neighborhood in Skokie was mixed Jewish and Catholic, and everybody got along just fine. I never lived in fear of catcalls or harassment and nobody ever threatened to harm me or beat me up.

All I knew about antisemitism was from Norman's stories. I was a typical kid, who didn't take the stories of their parent's childhood struggles seriously. "Yeah, right, dad," I used to say. "Whatever."

I had a cavalier attitude toward antisemitism. I didn't experience it, and I couldn't see it. I thought it had skipped a generation, or had disappeared completely in our modern world. I thought humanity had somehow matured and had outgrown it.

I was wrong, I learned later the hard way on my own. Norman telling stories about his own experiences with antisemitism prepared me for what I would encounter myself as an adult. I often wonder what Norman would have thought, if he still was alive today, about the recent rise in antisemitism.

Jews Don't Do That!

When I was a student at Northwestern trying to decide what to do with my life, I needed career advice. I was still in my antisemitism denial stage and was frustrated with Norman's answer to all my suggestions.

Norman always had the same answer. "Jews don't do that." I thought he was living in the past, where Jews were barred from just about every occupation. That just wasn't my reality.

I majored in political science and was interested in international affairs. I told Norman I wanted to sit for the Foreign Service exam. "Jews don't do that," was his answer. He was correct the State Department and many government agencies, like private businesses, didn't hire Jews. But that was in his day. By the time I took the exam in the 1970s, that just wasn't the case. The Foreign Service was open to all.

It was a moot point. I failed the exam, and that was the end of my stunning career as a diplomat.

He had the same answer for every other career idea I brought to him.

"Jews don't do that."

Exasperated, I finally asked, "So, dad, what do Jews do?"

"You can be anything you want," Norman replied, "as long as it's a doctor or a lawyer."

In Norman's day, and even long before, Jews have gravitated to medicine and law. They require a lot of education, something Jewish people value, and are portable, a hedge against volatile times, when Jews were bounced around from one European country to the next.

Since I couldn't stand the sight of blood, and I found law boring, medicine and law were out. I was turned down for medical and law school anyways, a sign those careers really weren't for me.

I ended up in journalism. "There aren't any Jews in newsrooms," Norman told me, after his usual, "Jews don't do that" refrain. Contrary to what Norman said, I found plenty of Jewish reporters, editors and other newsroom staff where I worked.

Norman's Least Favorite Rabbi

When Sara and I got engaged, Norman told us he had the perfect rabbi. I found this hard to believe, since Norman was a rebel. He simply just didn't get along, or like, most rabbis.

"I never met a rabbi I liked," Norman used to say.

The rabbi came from some well-to-do synagogue in Chicago. I'm not sure how Norman met or knew him, or why he liked him, but that's who Norman wanted to marry us. Sara and I found him distant and arrogant. We didn't particularly click with him. We weren't going to be bosom buddies. We just needed him to perform our wedding ceremony, so we went along.

Suddenly, a month before the wedding, he calls Norman and cancels, saying someone else "more important" in his synagogue was getting married the same day. We were all livid. Fortunately, Sara's mother, Eleanor, my mother-in-law to be, had a friend of a friend of a friend who knew Rabbi Aron Wolf of KAM Isaiah Israel Congregation in Hyde Park.

Rabbi Wolf was gracious enough to see us right away. Sara and her family were from Hyde Park, and I moved there to be with Sara after our engagement. He was quite a character himself. When we met him, he insisted we come to the next Friday night service. What was the topic of his sermon? Jewish divorce. A perfect topic for a young couple about to be married. Of course, he didn't tell us beforehand.

After Rabbi Wolf agreed to marry us, Norman and Sara and I ran into the rabbi who stood us up at Catch 35, an upscale fish restaurant downtown. He was having dinner with some big-busted blond *shiksa*, a Gentile woman, who apparently wasn't his wife.

The rabbi was a sitting duck for Norman. Still seething, Norman couldn't resist. He walked over to the rabbi. Norman went in for the kill.

"You know, rabbi," Norman said. "I don't recognize those tits." Norman turned the other way and walked right out of the restaurant, and never looked back.

The Accountant

"Money is the best gift.
It always fits."
-Norman

The Accountant

"I own a doorknob on that building."
-Norman pointing to an office building in Chicago

When Norman told Obama he was a Republican, he didn't mention he was an Eisenhower Republican. When he first told me, as a kid, I wasn't sure what he meant, since Norman often screwed up facts, even about well-known figures in American history.

I only figured it out later, as I watched times and politics changed around me, he meant Republicans focused on business, like Norman himself, not on culture wars and social issues. Norman was on top of the issues of his day – the Vietnam War, feminism, and civil rights, among others – he just didn't talk much about them, or start any discussions.

"When I walk in the office every morning," Norman used to say. "I say to myself, 'What's all this stuff got to do with my business?'" Norman didn't mix business with social causes. Business was business, and everything else was everything else, and Norman kept it that way.

Norman wasn't ideological. He was hard to pin down on the political spectrum. He could best be described as fiscally conservative but socially liberal. Then again, Norman wasn't rigid about anything. He adapted to change, rather than try to force his beliefs on others. He wasn't a debater, nor wanted to be. He wanted to get along with people, rather than get into fights.

Norman wasn't opinionated. He didn't hold strong views on anything or, at least, just kept them to himself.

If Norman disagreed with someone, he quietly listened and just said, "uh-huh," rather than get into an argument. That wasn't Norman's style. He waited until someone finished speaking and then moved on, or gently changed the subject.

"I'm just Archie Bunker," Norman joked, referring to the 70s sitcom about a blue-collar guy in Queens and his family, always with something to say, usually stanchly conservative and highly opinionated, about every issue of the day, social or political. The show was prophetic, decades ahead of its time, of the country's divide today between Red and Blue.

Norman wasn't Archie Bunker, at all. He wasn't as opinionated, or as conservative, as the fictional Mr. Bunker. It was just more nonsense Norman flung off the top of his head to get attention, or maybe just a laugh.

Norman was all business, just like his Grandpa Ike, who, coincidentally, had the same nickname as

Eisenhower. Maybe not so coincidental. Norman supported business-friendly policies – less government regulation and less taxes and was staunchly anti-union, also like his Grandpa Ike.

Norman may have been outrageous and crazy in public, but in private he was down-to-earth and a serious businessman. His accounting business was disciplined and organized. He was very detail oriented. He never missed a single line in any of his client's balance sheets or financial statements. He knew where every penny went, and where every penny was spent or saved and invested, always Norman's recommendation.

Norman was the same way with his own personal finances. He kept every receipt, every paid bill, every bank and brokerage statement in a top drawer in his desk.

Norman would also comment on my finances. Norman was a saver and investor. When he saw me spending too much, or not investing smartly, he used to say to me, "Let's go on a saving spree."

Norman wasn't flashy and didn't show off his few expensive possessions. He never wore a Rolodex someone once gave him as a gift. I didn't even know he owned one until I found it in a drawer after he died. Instead, Norman used to show off a simple plastic watch he bought at Walgreen's.

"This watch is great," he proudly told everybody.
"It only cost nine dollars at Walgreen's."

When the nine-dollar watch broke, he would send
it back to Timex for a replacement. He never had
to buy a new one. The nine-dollar watch had nine
lives.

Norman was a belt-and-suspenders accounting guy,
a CPA through and through. In another era,
Norman would have been the guy wearing a green
visor in the backroom hunched over accounting
ledgers and journals.

Norman was meticulous about every detail in the
latest tax code, which he read cover to cover. He
kept dog-eared copies of every annual tax code,
going back years, the heavy paperbacks, inches
thick, crammed onto his bookshelves, both at
home and the office.

Norman never threw away any tax code, even
when it all went online in his later years, and even
as they took up more and more space on his
shelves. He held on to them like gold. He never
knew when he might have to dig up an obscure tax
reg from the past for some client.

Norman's tax code library at home overpowered his
small den. It was larger than his collection of
coffee-table books about Chicago history and

architecture and his collection of blues and jazz CDs, his favorite music.

In his office, Norman had three-ring binders with bulletins from Commerce Clearing House (CCH), the leading news service about the latest tax legislation. In Norman's day, they were printed on tissue-thin paper and mailed to subscribers.

CCH bulletins were the tax accountant's gospel. They were always correct. Nobody ever questioned them – except Norman. He found an error in one page. He contacted CCH. They were stunned. The CCH never makes mistakes. They sent him a letter congratulating him.

Then, a few months later, Norman found a second error on another page. This time, the guy at CCH circled the error on the page, signed it and wrote underneath, "Flowers to you, Dubin!" and put it in a fancy black frame. Norman hung it proudly in his office like a big-game trophy.

Norman followed even the most obscure tax regulations like some people follow sports or celebrities.

On New Year's Eve, right after the clock struck midnight at Gibson's, where friends and family gathered every year, Norman would always mention how some bizarre new exemption, or tax rule, or whatever, had either just come into force, or had just expired. It was always arcane and off-the-wall. Nobody knew what he was talking about, and nobody paid attention. It was some secret lingo, an inside joke only understandable to accountants. It was just Norman being charming again, in his own eccentric way.

Norman's business allowed him to hobnob with some of Chicago's wealthiest people. He was a master at networking and had a thick Rolodex with not just business acquaintances but also people from all walks of life he happened to meet here and there, at the East Bank Club, restaurants, or wherever Norman was out and about.

Even with the elite, Norman wasn't afraid to crack a joke or two. A wealthy businessman from an exclusive real estate investment company on the West Coast, who Norman described as Waspy and serious, told Norman his ancestors came over on the Mayflower.

"I'll bet they were in cabin 2B," Norman told him at a business meeting. Norman told me the businessman, normally a bit of a stuffed shirt, laughed out loud at his quirky comment. Norman could lighten the façade of even the most serious people.

The Accountant

Whenever I needed someone for help, I went to Norman. He would chomp on his cigar and say, "I got a guy." He would spin his Rolodex and out would pop a name and a phone number. I was amazed at who he knew. Norman later replaced the Rolodex with an online directory, where he eventually moved all his contacts.

"Let me call this guy and tell him you're coming," Norman used to say. Norman opened doors for me, and others. He helped me, and others, get jobs. He helped people buy businesses, or find ones to startup. Norman was the connection. Norman knew everybody in Chicago. Norman was the guy to call. In the office, he was always on the phone. He was hard to reach during the day.

He was a wheeler-dealer, just like his Grandpa Ike.

Norman saw himself as a finance and numbers guy. He admired entrepreneurs, who he considered the heroes of the business world. He just felt he wasn't cut out to be one. He wasn't a risk taker.

"Accountants make terrible businessmen," Norman once told someone asking for advice how to run their business. He was the answer man about structuring financing but not about sales and marketing or management. He knew where accountants sat in the pecking order of the business world. He didn't overreach.

Norman respected great salespeople but didn't see himself as one. He believed great entrepreneurs, at their core, had to be great salespeople to succeed. Yet, his ability to network and make connections without hard selling was a great skill itself. He often just didn't see it in himself and always downplayed it.

Norman's CPA business still prospered. He did very well for himself, and Phyllis and I lived comfortably. We had no complaints. There was more than just bread on the table. There was lox and bagels, and sometimes also gefilte fish and prime rib. He lived in a luxury Lake Shore Drive condo building in one of Chicago's most exclusive neighborhoods on the North Side. He drove a BMW and was a member of the East Bank Club, an expensive rite of passage by itself.

Norman swam with big fish, Chicago's business elite, both Jewish and not, but couldn't play at their level. He was always the little guy, the fringe player, the silent partner with only a tiny sliver of the deal. He was just proud to be an investor, proud to be part of some action bigger than himself.

"I own a doorknob on that building," he said, pointing at a well-known office building he often walked by downtown. The multi-story skyscraper was valued at hundreds of millions of dollars and was owned by an investment group, of which Norman was a partner – a very small partner.

Norman used to tell people to buy at Walgreen's, not CVS. He never said why Walgreen's was the better drugstore. It just was, because Norman said so. He never said it was because he owned a block of shares of Walgreen's stock.

Norman had a mystical attachment to his cars. He held on to cars as long as ten years or until they clonked out in the street, whichever came first. He befriended mechanics who could miraculously resurrect his car back from the dead at the last minute. Maybe a jump here, maybe a new part there, maybe just a new battery or an oil change, or maybe just a tire rotation. Whatever it took. He had to hold on to his baby.

My car battery died one New Year's Eve right in front of their condo just as Sara and I were getting in the car to head to Gibsons. I frantically called Norman who was still upstairs. No problem. He knew just the guy, a Turkish mechanic he had befriended with a garage nearby. The mechanic towed the car to his shop nearby and replaced the battery, as I stood there in my tux near his oil cans.

Norman was always traumatized when he finally had to buy a new car. He would go all over town, to a dozen or more dealers, not sure what he should do.

Norman's soliloquy, "Should I or, shouldn't I?" drove dealers nuts as he kicked tires, test drove countless cars and paced around the showroom in a daze, looking up and down, mumbling to himself, and scratching his head, only to leave without buying anything, just as frustrated salespeople were about to toss him out of the store.

After Norman settled on a car, usually after ten or more visits to the same exhausted salesperson, the real pain began – his endless negotiations back and forth over the price and terms. He would chomp nervously on his cigar, as he spoke. They didn't wave goodbye as he drove off the lot. They were glad to be rid of him.

Of course, Norman didn't trade in his cherished old car. That was another ulcer. He had to sell it himself to be satisfied. No grubby dealer was going to put their dirty hands on his prized possession. He trembled as he signed the title over and stood outside, watching the new owner drive the car away. He waited until it was out of sight, then came in to grieve over his loss.

Norman in the Office: The Worker Bee

The Accountant

In the office, Norman was a worker bee. He called himself a *shveyr arbieter*, Yiddish, for a hard worker.

Norman had no tolerance for office politics or bullshit. He didn't crave power. He didn't bother other people in the office, or go around schmoozing. He just sat at his desk and worked. He minded his own business.

Norman was fiercely independent. With his experience, contacts, and knowledge, he got offers from clients to be a CFO or comptroller. He would have none of it. He didn't want to be under somebody else's thumb, especially some ego-driven or powerful CEO. He and his partner, Marshall, only merged their practice with a big firm to get more staff as their business expanded.

Norman and Marshall came in at a partner level to Philip Rootberg Company, a local Chicago accounting firm, later acquired by CBIZ, a much bigger national accounting and business consulting practice.

Norman's biggest sacrifice when he merged with Rootberg was giving up his chewed-up cigar. The office was smoke-free.

Norman wasn't the most powerful partner, nor did he want to be.

But to the army of young associates, Norman was the most approachable partner. I called him the office's Father Confessor. When not on the phone, wheeling and dealing or talking to clients, he was mentoring some associate. His door was always open. New hires would open up to him, whether about their work or about a difficult client or, sometimes, even just a personal struggle.

Norman relished his role as a mentor to the young staff. During the infamous tax season from February to April, when CPAs work into the night seven days a week to get tax returns filed on time, a young associate once came into Norman's office crying. She was stressed about the excessive work load. Norman calmed her down and helped her get back to work.

Norman knew how to talk to people, even when he had to be serious. He was the same inside the office, except without his usual hijinks, as he was outside the office. He just knew how to connect with people, whether the elite or just the ordinary guy.

Norman gave his all to his clients. He was totally client-focused. When he died, CBIZ ran a half-page ad with Norman's picture in Crain's, the leading Chicago business weekly, thanking him for his outstanding service to both the firm and his clients.

The Accountant

He may have only been a legend in his own mind, but to his clients he was legendary.

Norman loved to work. He didn't have any hobbies other than going to his usual haunts and running around town. He tried golf once, because it was what businessmen did when he was young, but the clubs lost their shine, gathering a thick layer of dust hidden under the stairs in the basement of his Skokie house. He knew he would just chop up the golf course, if he had to use his clubs.

"What I do wouldn't be golfing," Norman said. "It would be landscaping."

When Norman reached the age where the firm put partners out to pasture, he still had a full roster of big revenue clients, so they kept him on. They moved him out of his office with a picture window overlooking the river into a small windowless office down the hall and out of sight.

"They put me in a broom closet," Norman used to say. It didn't stop Norman. He kept working as hard as ever. He just had to cram all his tax books from his bigger office into a bookshelf right on top of him in the smaller office.

Norman never retired. He worked until just a month before he died, when he was too sick to come into the office. He died with his boots on.

The Finale

"He was so handsome when he picked me up on that first date."
-Phyllis looking at Norman on life support

The Finale

"Nobody is going to visit me."
-Phyllis about the cemetery plots

Norman was never late to a restaurant. This time
he was almost an hour late. He came in without
Phyllis. Where was Phyllis? They were inseparable.
They never missed a dinner outing on the weekend
together. How could he forget to bring her?

I knew something was up when I stepped outside
Gene & Georgetti and thought I had seen Norman
drive by, alone, in MAZLTOV and then drive off. The
valet said he had seen the same thing. He said he
also had seen Norman pass by and leave. He said it
wasn't my imagination.

Then Norman showed up. He was still without
Phyllis. He said she wasn't ready. What? That
couldn't be, I thought. Phyllis was always
meticulous. She was always put together, and
always put together on time. What was going on?

Norman sat down at the table with Sara and I and
ordered breakfast. The normally chatty Mexican
waiter was silent. He just looked at Norman poker-
faced. No cute Yiddish expressions tonight.

"But, dad, it's dinner time," I said.

"I thought it was the morning," Norman said. "I want breakfast. I'll have two eggs."

Norman took out a credit card. The waiter came back. It was declined. I looked at the card. It had expired. He found another card – this one valid – and paid the bill.

Norman was always sharp. Goofy, inarticulate, yes, but always on his game. He could say the craziest things. He could embarrass me in public to no need. But, underneath, he knew exactly where he was and what he was doing.

I had never seen Norman like this.

I was scared and the next two weeks made me even more scared.

Norman's lifelong illness had finally caught up with him. He had a congenital heart defect, Bicuspid Aortic Valve (BAV) disease. The valve of the aorta, the heart's largest artery, has three leaflets. The aortic valve of BAV sufferers only has two leaflets. It's the most common congenital heart ailment. Norman's case was typical, not something for the medical journals.

Norman knew about it since his childhood. It, obviously, didn't stop him from living a rich life. He mentioned it only once in passing, saying he got a

4-F medical exemption from military service during the Korean War.

Norman never talked about it, so I never thought about it. It wasn't until he really got sick, I figured out why he always had an obsession with cardiology. I never understood why he would be interested in such an arcane subject totally outside his wheelhouse.

It wasn't until he was in his late 70s doctors noticed some stress on his aorta. The valve was wearing out and needed to be replaced. Norman went to several cardiologists to get a second opinion. They were unanimous. The valve needed to be replaced.

Norman came through the surgery just fine. He was in good health and excellent shape. Racquetball and working out at the East Bank Club paid off. The club was more than just a pitstop for mingling and girl watching. He was even back on the racquetball court a few years later when he turned 80. He was back to being his old goofy self.

The replacement valve held up for a few years, then started showing signs of wear. The doctors put him on Warfarin, a powerful blood thinner, once also used as a rat poison. I had no idea, until it was too late, how much it had damaged Norman's mind. I didn't even know he was on medication. He never told me.

Norman slowly started to decline. I didn't notice. He hid it well. He was still functioning, still working and going to the office, still running around and still eating out. As far as I could tell, nothing had changed. Sara kept telling me something wasn't right with Norman. She said he just wasn't himself. I thought she was seeing things.

That was until the incident at Gene & Georgetti. I started to notice he was losing control. He was talking nonsense. It wasn't his normal kidding around anymore. Something was different, very different. I didn't want to admit it to myself. He might have dementia. It was unthinkable in such a bright guy with a sharp mind and an even sharper wit.

Then his office started calling me.

"Where's Norman? He hasn't been to the office in weeks. What's going on?" I didn't know either, I answered. I had to find out myself. Norman suddenly went from eccentric to mysterious.

Norman's doctor wouldn't talk to me. Norman had only authorized Phyllis, not me, as the point of contact. He was missing appointments, either on purpose, or because he simply forgot.

The same for his bank. He left Phyllis to write the checks and pay the bills. Like the doctor, he hadn't authorized me to sign checks.

Part of Norman's business was estate planning, mostly for wealthy individuals and trust fund "brats," as he used to call them. Everything was in order. All the paperwork was ready. I just wasn't on any accounts or powers of attorney. He had set up everything only for Phyllis. He must have assumed she would be competent and have all her faculties. It turned out, she didn't.

Phyllis wasn't all there either, I suddenly realized. She was starting to lose it. Apparently, she was also on the road to dementia. On top of that, Phyllis couldn't walk any more. She had recently started using a walker to get around.

It was a frightening scenario. One I never expected. Two half demented people, one also disabled, running the show and trying to take care of the house together. They had just hired a caregiver to help them. The situation was far worse than I had expected.

I arranged for Phyllis to meet me at the doctor's and banker's offices. I put her and her walker and caregiver in taxis. It was a ghastly scene escorting Phyllis in her walker in downtown office buildings, navigating elevators and unforgiving crowds.

The Finale

The only thing still holding up was Phyllis's beehive. The fiberglass kept her hair in place. Nothing could take that baby down. Not even Chicago's strong lakefront winds, from which it gets its nickname as The Windy City.

The doctor gave her office permission to give me information, and the banker gave me authority to sign checks. It was just in time. Phyllis was about to write a check from an empty account. The banker transferred some of his savings into the checking account, then added me to those accounts as well. Finally, things were back to normal. Sort of.

I called Angelo and told him something was wrong with Norman. He and Olga, and Sara and I, visited Norman at his condo. Norman was babbling some nonsense. Phyllis wasn't much help. She was making bizarre comments all over the map.

Angelo and Olga helped me take away Norman's car keys. He didn't protest or stop us. I don't think he fully knew what we were doing.

A few days later on Saturday, I visited the condo. Norman was sitting in bed, fully clothed and fully awake, on blood-stained sheets. Blood-soaked Kleenexes were on the floor. His nose had been bleeding on and off that morning.

"It's nothing," Norman said. "It's just a little nose bleed. It'll pass."

I was about to call an ambulance, when I realized they would only take him to Saint Joseph a few blocks away. He didn't want to go there. He wanted to go to Northwestern, where all his doctors were. I called a neighbor, who was kind enough to drive him downtown.

In the emergency room, a doctor asked some stock questions to check his mental state.

"Who is the president?" the doctor asked.

"I don't know," Norman said. "But I think his wife his Black." Norman had even forgotten the name of his naked locker room buddy from the East Bank Club, who was then the president.

"Where are we now?" the doctor continued.

"Cleveland," Norman said. Why Cleveland? There was a famous heart center there. Norman probably had looked at going there for treatment, and it must have been on his mind, what was left of it.

Norman ended up in the hospital for a week. It was quite a week. He had lost his mind and was yelling at nurses and telling everybody he was going to sue them. Sara and I visited him only once. It was an unforgettable experience.

"Stupid, stupid, stupid, stupid, son," Norman yelled at me. "Where have you been?"

I just swallowed it. It was the dementia talking, not Norman. I knew it wasn't what he really felt in his heart, injured as it was. It was coming from some other place, only God knew where. Until now, I couldn't have had a better PR department than Norman. Even if a bit embellished, at times, he was always in my corner, always tooting my horn.

Northwestern sent him for rehab to Warren Barr, a nearby nursing home. It was on a Friday. Sunday, they called me. He had only been there two days. He was running a fever and had to be taken back to the hospital.

Sara and I rushed back over to the emergency room that night. I was in shock. It wasn't just a fever. He was on life support in intensive care. He was on a respirator, all kinds of unnamed tubes going in and out of every possible opening in his body, it seemed. I was too upset to keep track. His eyes were closed, and he was unconscious. I couldn't bear to look at him in this state.

The Finale

Phyllis insisted on visiting him in intensive care. It was heartbreaking. Hunched over the walker, her gnarled hands gripping the handles, she tried to talk to Norman. She told the story of how handsome he was when he picked her up at her parent's house for their first date in high school. He probably didn't hear her. I was choked up and on the verge of tears.

It tore my heart apart to see Norman, such a vigorous and vibrant man, full of life and fun, in a vegetative state hooked up to machines and monitors.

Phyllis never saw Norman again. Two weeks later, we met with his doctor in a closed room in intensive care. The young doctor put his hand on Phyllis's arm. He looked sadly at her and said he was sorry. There was nothing more they could do, he told her. He had congestive heart failure and couldn't breathe unaided. His lungs were full of fluid. I had also noticed the bag collecting his urine was now filled with red fluid. It was blood. I knew the end was near.

Norman had to be moved to hospice, they told her. I knew that was a death sentence. Off the respirator, it was only a matter of time. Phyllis and I had no choice.

The Finale

Sara and I were in the elevator on our way to Northwestern's hospice facility when the call came. Norman had just passed away moments ago. When I got there, I opened the door a crack. Norman's head was cocked to the side, resting on his shoulder. He looked like he was asleep. That's the image I wanted to keep of him in my mind, like he was just resting after a game at the East Bank Club. I signed some paperwork, and then left.

Word of Norman's passing ricocheted through his condo building within hours. I had only called one neighbor, and the informal phone tree went into action.

The day before the funeral, Sara and I downloaded his contact list. As expected, there were hundreds of names. We just divided up the list and started calling people like crazy. It took us all day and into the night. I know we missed a few people here and there. But we got to his most cherished friends and family and, of course, his office and business associates.

Norman's funeral was in the biggest room at Weinstein Funeral Home in Wilmette, just north of the border with Skokie, where we had once lived. The room was packed. Kenny, the owner of Manny's, and my Uncle Ronnie, "The Admiral," were both there and surprised to be mentioned in my eulogy.

The Finale

Countless family and friends from over the years, surviving members of his college fraternity and their spouses, and even a contingent from his office were all there.

When I told the infamous Obama story in the eulogy, I threw in a comment how Norman would have been glad to know people had a laugh or two at his funeral. Just as in life, he didn't want to be taken too seriously. If he had his way, he would have had a party for his send off. He would have wanted people to have fun, not to be sad.

Norman and Sid, my father-in-law, had bought a set of six plots for the two families at Memorial Park in Skokie, coincidentally, only a few years before. My mother-in-law Eleanor hadn't been well for a while, and Sara's family suggested buying the plots. Her family wanted to be prepared. Who knew Norman would come up suddenly from the rear and beat her to the finish line. Who knew he, not Eleanor, would be the first inhabitant.

Buying the plots was like shopping for a condo. Memorial Park's small administration building had the look and feel of a sales center for real estate instead of a cemetery office. We leafed through big picture albums with lovely landscapes of well-manicured lawns and neatly trimmed trees.

The Finale

We also purchased a stone bench engraved with our family's names. "Why did you get that?" Phyllis said, a little pissed off. "Nobody is going to visit me." Ever the Jewish mother, she felt abandoned, even in the cemetery.

The cemetery, besides being in Norman's least favorite place, suburban Skokie, was right across the street from Norman's least favorite shopping center, Old Orchard. At least the graves were near the front in a bright and open area. It was sunny during good weather and cheerful or, at least, as cheerful as a cemetery could be.

Eleanor was too sick to attend Norman's funeral and died three weeks to the day later. Her funeral was also at Weinstein, and the funeral director looked at the audience and said, "I see some familiar faces here from last time."

It was a surreal summer dealing with the back-to-back passing only weeks apart of two family members. I was so on edge, whenever I answered the phone, I screamed hysterically, "Who died?"

The cemetery, like the funeral home, was full of cars with people paying their respects.

The woman my father called "a sexy broad" was there. I reminded her of what Norman said. She remembered and laughed.

The Finale

Angelo and Olga were there. Olga pointed at the Greek section of the cemetery just behind the Jewish area where Norman was buried. "We're going to be over there," Olga said, trying to comfort me, in an odd sort of way, they would someday be Norman's neighbors for eternity.

Norman was buried wrapped in a cloth *tallit*, a Jewish prayer shawl, I had bought for him in Jerusalem.

The Shiva, the visitation after a Jewish funeral, at the condo was equally as well attended. It lasted two long days. I was exhausted and amazed at the number of people who knew Norman and came to express their condolences. It was a lot for Phyllis to deal with. But she held up. For a moment her dementia abated, and she was gracious with everyone.

Kathy from Gibson's personally delivered a table of food, setting it up in the hallway just outside the condo. Another cousin left her credit card number on my voice mail and said, "Just go ahead and get a tray for Norman." It's a Jewish tradition to bring, or order, a tray of food for a Shiva.

Sheldon from Gibson's was greeted at the condo by a doorman, who also happened to be Black. He told the doorman he was my half-brother. The doorman looked at him funny before letting him come up.

We had "He loved Chicago" with a Chicago flag engraved on his headstone.

I could have sworn I saw Norman in the distance waving goodbye at the grave site during the ceremony. Maybe it was a mirage. Maybe not. Maybe he was waving at the city he loved, the city which loved him back. Maybe he was waving at the many, many people whose lives he touched.

Norman would remain an indelible memory in the minds of his family, his countless friends, his business acquaintances, and the random strangers he encountered and made laugh.

I was deeply fortunate to have had Norman in my life as my father and best friend for fifty-five years. Norman would remain in my heart forever.

Sometimes, I think Norman is still looking down on me from that East Bank Club in the sky.

"I'm proud of you, kid."

Epilogue

"I hear you just fine!
I don't need a hearing aide."
-Phyllis

Epilogue

"We're keeping an eye on your mother."
"Oh, she's so sweet."
-Residents and staff at Phyllis's nursing home

After Norman passed away, Phyllis steadily declined both mentally and physically. By now, she was completely housebound at the condo. She was confined to a wheelchair and, when she had to get up, could only get around with a walker.

Phyllis also now needed help with everything. When Norman died, I had to transfer the credit cards, among other things to her and me. A credit card company, who will remain unnamed, insisted Phyllis be on the phone. She squawked, "What's she asking?" at every question from the customer service rep. I said to Phyllis, "Just say, 'yes,' mom."

After the phone call, I got a letter a week later from the card company, expressing condolences on the death of "Joel Dubin." After ninety minutes on the phone, I thought they could have gotten the name of the deceased right. I called them back and said, "I'm Joel Dubin, and I'm not dead yet, but I think you're trying to kill me." The rep read some canned nonsense from a script apologizing for the inconvenience.

Sara and I still tried to keep taking her out on weekends, but only to Gibsons and Gene &

Georgetti, her only two restaurants with wheelchair
access. Between maneuvering the wheelchair and
then packing her up in the car and the confusion
from dementia, it just became too difficult to bring
her anywhere.

Gradually, her memory slipped deeper into
dementia, and she stopped asking to go out.

All that remained were her beehive hairdo, slowly
deflating as she aged, and her strong lungs, intact
enough to still unexpectedly throw a verbal dagger
out of the dark.

"I can hear you just fine," Phyllis screeched, when
her doctor said she needed a hearing aid. "I don't
need a hearing aid."

Phyllis once escaped from the condo in the middle
of the night. Somehow, she unlocked the door, got
into the elevator unnoticed, and snuck through a
back door of the building past the doorman and his
surveillance camera.

The police spotted her, strolling down Sheridan
Road behind the condo building. They couldn't
have missed her, an elderly woman in her late 80s
in a daze, barefoot and wearing only a nightgown.

They took her to Saint Joseph hospital nearby,
where, coincidentally, her doctor's office was also

located. She was lucid enough to give the emergency room her name. They found my number in her doctor's records and called me at 4:30 in the morning and told me to pick up my mother.

I was very, very lucky the police and the hospital got to Phyllis right away. It could have been a lot worse.

It was obvious. Phyllis needed skilled nursing care. She was becoming too much for the caregiver to handle. By now, she was completely unaware of her surroundings and had even forgotten my name. The once feisty Jewish mother, whose screams could shatter glass, was frighteningly silent.

I found a small intimate nursing home near us in Skokie. Sara and I had moved back to the ancestral homeland a few years after Norman died.

I was a total wreck the day Phyllis moved to the nursing home. I stood in the lobby of the condo building and cried uncontrollably as the driver wheeled her into the medical van. It killed me to see her taken from her home of nearly forty years to an anonymous place where she was a total stranger.

Phyllis was calm. She had to be. She had no idea what was going on. I regained my composure as I followed the van for the half-hour drive north on Lake Shore Drive, into Edgewater, down Peterson Avenue and up Lincoln Avenue through Lincolnwood and finally into Skokie. Phyllis would never see the city she and Norman loved again.

When we got to the nursing home, I thanked the driver for his patience – he said she was totally calm the whole trip – and gave him a generous tip. I guess I had inherited Norman's membership into The Golden Tipper's Club.

A welcoming committee warmly greeted Phyllis in the lobby. Everybody was so warm and friendly. I knew I had made the right decision. Phyllis smiled, unaware where she was, and quietly said her first words of the day under her breath. "Nice to meet everybody." I think she thought she was on a cruise or in a resort.

I visited her the next day. The staff clearly had been attentive and helpful. She just smiled at me and pulled my cheek close to her lips and kissed me. She never said my name again. She repeated this ritual whenever I visited every few days. I think she knew who I was or, at least, I wanted to believe she still recognized her son.

The first time I visited, after she got settled in a few days later, she was sitting in the day room with all the other residents. "We're keeping an eye on your mother," a woman in the wheelchair next to my Phyllis said. Oddly, her name was also Phyllis.

I just said, "OK." I didn't realize there was a gang in the nursing home. I didn't dare lift up her sleeve, but I pictured a tattoo on her shoulder with an arrow through a heart, saying, "The Elder Babes. Hell Can Wait." It turns out, I learned, the other Phyllis was, in fact, the heavy in the day room. If anybody needed anything, they had to go through her. She would yell at the staff and get results. There was no messing with Phyllis number two.

One of the nurses told me, "Oh, your mother is so sweet." I guess she somehow missed the first eighty years of Phyllis's screaming and yelling.

A Russian social worker at the home recognized Phyllis's maiden name, Brodsky, and took her under her wing. Apparently, Brodsky was the name of a famous Soviet poet, and she thought Phyllis might have been related, since Phyllis's family, like Norman's, had Russian Jewish roots dating back to the 1800s. It turned out they weren't from the same Brodsky family. It didn't matter. The social worker still treated Phyllis like royalty.

Just before Covid hit, the small intimate nursing home in Skokie was bought by a chain of north suburban nursing homes. Phyllis was moved to the

Northbrook facility, and the Skokie home was turned into the chain's Covid ward.

I didn't see Phyllis again in person after that. The nursing home arranged for weekly FaceTime calls. It made a big difference. I was, at least, able to see her, even though all she did was stare blankly and silently into the phone without smiling. Again, I may have been deluding myself, but I think she recognized me. I'll never know.

In a rare lucid moment, Phyllis asked me where Norman was. She had forgotten he had passed. It had to tell her. "Norman died a few years ago." It was pitiful. She cried. It tore at my heart.

Then right during the second peak of Covid in November 2020, I got the call. Phyllis had Covid. She was being moved back to the Skokie facility. I cried nonstop for four days. I knew she wasn't going to make it. She was already 91 years old and was very weak.

I got the second call early Saturday morning, while I was out running. The nursing home just left a message on my voice mail, telling me to call back. I called back. She had stopped breathing at 5:15 in the morning.

Due to Covid restrictions, Phyllis didn't have a funeral. Only someone from the funeral home and my closest childhood friend, Peter, were at the grave site, as she was quietly buried next to Norman. I wrote a eulogy that was never read. There was nobody present to hear it.

Phyllis died alone. It reminded me of the Beatles song, Eleanor Rigby, where no one came to her funeral and the priest wiped his hands as he walked away from the grave. For Phyllis, it was the funeral director, leaving the cemetery after an impromptu brief service no one attended.

The Norman and Phyllis Show was finally over. Their playful craziness would now only be a memory.

I had Phyllis's tombstone engraved with "Just a Small Town Cookie," what she told everybody about her Joliet roots.

Sara and I still went to some of Norman's favorite restaurants. With time, that tapered off, especially as we moved north back to Skokie. In true Norman style, we had our own markers at our own restaurants, some in the city, some in the suburbs.

We took a friend once to a restaurant in Greek Town on Halsted. Everybody knew me there. In typical Norman style, the Assyrian valet guys from Iraq didn't have to give me a ticket. They all knew the crazy Jewish guy from Skokie who spoke Arabic.

Epilogue

There was a two-hour wait. I spoke a few sentences in my broken Greek, and the maître d' gestured, "Wait on the side. Just five minutes."

Sure enough, the three of us were seated in five minutes. Our friend said, "It's good to be with Tony Soprano." Norman would have been proud.

In another postscript to Norman's life, one of the Mexican waiters, told me after Norman died, Norman's broken Yiddish lessons made him curious about the Jewish people and inspired him to visit Israel.

I always said if insanity was hereditary, I was in trouble.

I was every bit of Norman's son – the networker, the comedian, the fixer – the silent power broker who always can still make them laugh.

I was every bit of Phyllis's son – the smart aleck with the quick answer to even the dumbest questions.

Insanity maybe not, but Norman's car, MAZLTOV, I inherited, for sure.

Going south down Lake Shore Drive in MAZLTOV past the Taste, I still feel Norman and Phyllis in the back seat. Phyllis is yelling at Norman about something, and Norman is ignoring her. Instead, he is looking over my shoulder.

"Take a right on Roosevelt, kid," Norman whispers in my ear, stashing his chewed-up cigar in a plastic bag by his side. "We need to stop at Manny's."

The Norman
and Phyllis Show
Photo Album

"Phyllis's hair looks perfect in every picture."
-Sara

Norman's Grandparents
Celia and Ike Wedding in Chicago 1903

Norman and Phyllis's Wedding 1951:
From Left: Grandma Ida, Norman, Phyllis,
Grandma Brandy (Celia), Grandpa Ike,
Cousin Stuart

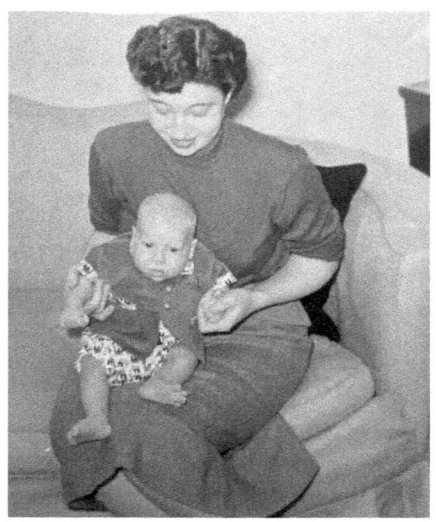

Phyllis and me at four months old in 1957

Norman and Phyllis in the 1950s

Phyllis Pre-Beehive 1940s
Norman: "She was so sexy back then!"

Norman on left, David on the right in the 1940s

David, Norman and Angelo Reunited in the 1980s

Grandma Ida's Third Marriage to Sam in St. Paul
She was 73 years old

Phyllis with Her Mother, Grandma Ethel 1980s

Norman and Phyllis
Her Beehive Through the Years

Norman at Seder at East Bank Club
From Left: Norman, Sid, Eleanor, Sara

Angelo and Olga

Sid and Eleanor
Sara and I

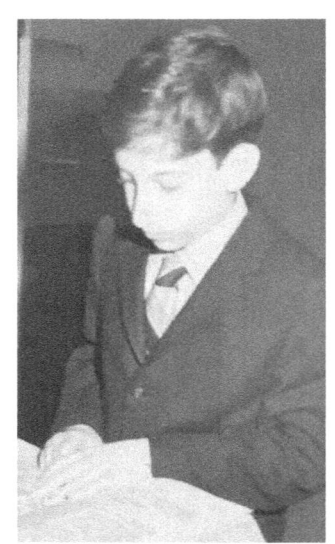

My Bar Mitzvah 1970

Norman as TV Detective Columbo

www.ingramcontent.com/pod-product-compliance
Lightning Source LLC
Chambersburg PA
CBHW061724120626
46550CB00005B/1702